Moments This Good

Bonnie Nester is author of two short stories in the Chicken Soup series published by Health Communications, Inc.

"Fishing Patriots" (also in this volume as "Patriotic Fishermen") appeared in *Chicken Soup for the Fisherman's Soul.*

"Poor Clyde" appeared in *Chicken Soup for the Soul in Menapause.*

Moments This Good

The Softer Side of Alzheimer's

~~~~~~~~~~

A Memoir of
Hope and
Love

By:
Bonnie Nester

*Enjoy every moment —
Bonnie Nester*

Golden Quill Publishing
Hillsboro, Oregon

Bonnie Nester 18695 Holznagel Rd
Sherwood, Oregon 97140
503.625.7828 www.BonnieNester.com

Shown on front cover: Ruth Zora and Jerry Lasselle.
Some names within have been changed to protect the
privacy of individuals and families.

A portion of the proceeds from sales of this book is
donated to the Alzheimer's Association.

Front cover design by Jeri Owen.
Interior design by Sherry Green.

14 13 12 11 10 09 08 1 2 3 4 5 6 7

ISBN 13: 978–0–9802446–0–1
ISBN 10: 0–9802446–0–9

Printed in the United States of America.
Printed on acid-free paper.

To my mother

—for all she taught me, though
I didn't truly learn to appreciate
and understand her strength and
wisdom until these last years of
her life.

Ruth

 From Mom's Journal:

> *Cast me not off in the time of
> old age; forsake me not when my
> strength faileth.*
>
> —Psalm 71:9

Table of Contents

Acknowledgements

My first acknowledgement is for my husband Jim who stood beside me and Mom through these difficult years of Alzheimer's disease. He respected her as he steadied her and held her arm going down the stairs. He complimented her even as he helped her from the car, teasing her about her hair and going dancing, letting her be the woman she was, as long as she could be. He understood and comforted me on the days I came home crying, the days I was angry or frustrated with Mom's care, and the many days I simply grieved for the loss of my mother. He never resented the time I spent with Mom and her needs, as well as the hours spent at the computer working on my stories. I thank him too, for using his woodworking talent to honor Mom. It was only fitting that he would handcraft the beautiful cedar box that held her ashes as we sent her off at journey's end.

Appreciation goes to my family who knew the writing was helping me get through the time of acceptance and moments of laughter, frustration, and grieving. They all loved Mom so much. I hope this book honors that love. I know they each have stories of their own.

So much respect and thanks are given to my many "critiquers" of the www.INK writing group. Paulie Tietz, Gail Johnson, Julie Kepler, Pam Rosales, Shirley Dechaine, and Jeannie Unger were the core group when I started with my project. Those and others who attended helped me so much. They laughed and cried with me as the book took form, and I'm sure I wouldn't have finished it without their love and encouragement.

A special thanks goes to Carrie Richards and Joan Cairns who read the first draft adding many commas, words, and helpful suggestions.

My thanks also to the women from my bible study group at Countryside Church who prayed for me and helped me work through the hard times after Mom died when I couldn't write and was ready to quit and shelve the whole idea of a book. Group leaders Mary Kerkanich and Julie Tannehill will always hold a special place in my heart.

No writing project is completed without editor and publisher. Linda Meyer, my editor, seemed to know my heart with her first reading of the manuscript. She was so kind and clear with her suggestions. Sherry Green, my publisher, was an ever-present force. She convinced me that the book had value and held information that needed to be shared. She is certainly an important person to whom I owe the will to finally see the project to completion.

I give a special thank you to my friend Jeri Owen, who saw me stop and start more than once. As we spent time in my basement craft room, she let me vent and then was supportive when I picked up the project again. Her friendship and her skill with the cover design were invaluable.

My thanks to the Alzheimer's Association for the help and information they provided. A special appreciation for Judy McKellar and the understanding she shared from her own experiences, having lost both parents to Alzheimer's.

I must also acknowledge all those incredible caregivers who spend their lives doing what so many of us can't do. They are an amazing group of people. A special caregiver named Susan will always have my heartfelt gratitude for the effort she made to personalize her care for Mom while she was at the Avamere in Sherwood.

And to the many families and friends I was privileged to meet along this journey, I say thank you. Hold strong and grab all the precious memories your hearts can hold.

Publisher's note: many quotations within this book have been drawn from unattributed entries in Ruth Zora's journal. We have done our utmost to track down the source of the quotations, but when it was not possible, we have printed them as Ruth copied them, since the main purpose of this book is to document the withering of her lively mind. We will appreciate corrections and include them in any second edition of this book.

Ruth's confirmation at age 13.

1

I can still hear my Aunt Gladys saying, "You take good care of Ruthie, now. She's very special to this family, you know."

I do know.

Ruth Matilda Samuelson, my mother, was born on May 9, 1916, in Superior, Wisconsin. The middle child of Swedish immigrant parents, she was a favorite of her four siblings. No matter what her age, when asked who her best friend was, Ruth would likely reply "my sisters" or "my brother." Young Ruth was outgoing and friendly, a tomboy continually in motion. She could be seen balancing on the railroad tracks pretending to be a tightrope walker. A stroll down the sidewalk might turn into cartwheels or waltzing with an imaginary partner. She was adventurous and envisioned herself being a world traveler someday.

Yes, we would heed Aunt Gladys's loving admonishment to take care of Ruthie. Despite losing a baby to Sudden Infant Death Syndrome (SIDS), having her home and possessions burn to the ground, and surviving divorce and the deaths of two husbands, my mother was unprepared for what was to come. At the age of eighty, Ruth faced the most challenging journey of her life: Alzheimer's disease.

Ruth was not afraid of challenges or hard work. After our family migration to Oregon, she willingly did whatever it took to make ends meet. As a child, I remember her saying, "There is such an abundance of food here in Oregon. If anyone starves in this country, they've only themselves to blame." The farm our family rented was across the road from the Birdseye strawberry fields, and soon we were all involved in harvesting berries. The days were long, hot, and dusty. Food growers regularly needed help with the harvest. After the strawberries there were blackcaps, cucumbers, green beans, and prunes, then filberts and walnuts to pick. Mom particularly seemed to enjoy being outside in the warm days of Indian summer while picking filberts in the huge shady orchards. Later, as opportunities arrived, she worked in the local canneries, finally being "paid by the hour." However, after our stepfather became ill with cancer, she realized she needed more than seasonal work.

She applied for a posted dietitian's position at a private Portland mental hospital, as such facilities were then known, even though the only experience she had was that of cooking for farmhands in Montana and subbing in the cafeteria at the small school we attended. Surprisingly, she was hired. Ruth told her new employer she couldn't start for a week, and later that day came home from the library with an armload of books about food allergies and special diets. Her work was often highly praised.

Success in her first dietitian's job gave her the confidence to apply for other hospital work when that facility closed down. She used her experience to find jobs in psychiatric hospitals in Oregon, Wisconsin, and Montana. If a position were unavailable in the kitchen, she took a job in another area of the hospital, often as a caregiver. Ruth had an especially soft place in her heart for the Downs Syndrome children abandoned in psychiatric hospitals in those days. She remarked often how "the kids" generally seemed happy and smiling. I remember her saying, "Maybe they are the lucky ones."

When my sister Marge's son was born frail and unable to gain weight, the doctors diagnosed his problem as celiac disease. They said he wouldn't live past his sixth birthday. Not one to accept defeat, Mom made her way to the library again. She studied everything she could about treatment or cure of this disease, but it was an uncommon problem and not much information was available at the time. Ruth learned that bananas and skim milk were easily digested, and so The Campaign began. I've never seen so many bananas eaten by one small baby. He may have been misdiagnosed, or, with a strong will, he may have lived anyway. But according to our family, Ruth made the difference. To her, it was nothing more than any grandmother would do for a sickly grandchild. That scrawny little boy grew into a strong young man who served with the Marines in Vietnam. Unfortunately, the war took a toll on John, emotionally and physically. He was struck down by a heart attack at the age of forty-one.

Mom was proud of John's service to his country and that of another grandson, Wes. Her brother had served in the navy during World War II, and she was quite patriotic. She proudly served in the VFW auxiliary later in her life, while married to her third husband, Joe Zora.

There was a spontaneous side to Ruth that might take her off to Reno with a bag of quarters she'd been stashing, or on a quick trip to Montana or Wisconsin to see family. She lived in many states throughout her life, but all she needed was what she could fit into a car. She put little value in possessions— furnishings could be replaced. When we were younger, she occasionally took us out of school for short trips, justifying them as educational. Her restless spirit stayed with her all her life. Friends and family joked about Ruth having "gypsy blood" because of her love for travel.

Ruth with her brother Harry, in the early 1940's. Though she was two years older than him, as an adult, he would often refer to her as his "Little Buddy."

When she visited a new town, Ruth's first stops were the Chamber of Commerce and the library to familiarize herself with the area. She loved books. A year after being diagnosed with Alzheimer's, following a stop at the library with my sister, she commented, "This is a good information place. Can I get a room here?"

Even as Mom's trips became less frequent and she gave up driving her car, she still didn't slow down. Her adventures were just on a smaller scale. She enjoyed using public transportation. She'd be off on the city bus, heading downtown for lunch or to visit a daughter. Not afraid to talk to anyone, Mom usually found interesting conversation. No bus ride was too long or too complicated if she was on a mission. When the family worried aloud about her safety, she refused to be intimidated.

Ruth was open-minded, generous of spirit, and had a heart for the underdog. Her insatiable curiosity and zest for life left us unprepared for her impending battle with Alzheimer's disease. We learned that for an Alzheimer's patient there is no typical profile and no predictable traits. Each case is unique. Her reality and ours changed as we struggled our way through it with her.

I asked myself, *How did she get to Alzheimer's disease? When did this terrible illness begin? Did that hard fall on the ice have anything to do with it?* I can't recall the day I saw the changes begin. Was there a time when Mom thought to herself, *What is happening to me? Why do I feel confused, and why is life becoming so difficult?* I do not know. I never will.

Our family was shocked and a little dismayed when at the age of seventy-three, Mom announced that she and the social worker she had contacted had decided she should move into an assisted living facility called The Heritage. It seemed a strange decision for one so independent. She'd told us earlier that she didn't want to live with her children in her later years. Mom did not want to be a burden...but assisted living? Her reasoning was sound. She would still be able to come and go as she pleased. It would be nice to have meals cooked and laundry done. To us it just didn't seem like Mom's style. Too regimented.

After each visit with Mom in her new apartment, I cried all the way home. I could not accept my mother living in a place filled with sad, tired, gray faces. My happy-go-lucky, independent, and active mother was out of place there. My siblings agreed. However, when she needed knee surgery shortly after the move, we saw the wisdom of her decision. Caregivers, cooks, housekeepers, and physical therapists were there to help her. Most importantly, she kept her independence.

As years passed, the family noticed other changes in our mother's behavior and attitude. She began calling me to come and find her purse, invariably "hidden" on top of her cupboards. Paranoia is an early symptom of Alzheimer's disease, though of course we didn't recognize it as such. She called to say her sleeping medication was gone, sure that it had been stolen. In her mind there was someone she called "Miss Sticky Fingers" taking things from her room. After repeated incidents, we decided to have Mom's medications mailed directly to the nurse's station at The Heritage. When we cleaned out the medicine cabinet in her room, it was quite revealing to find several over-the-counter medicines, outdated medicines, previously prescribed medicines, and, most surprising, other people's medicines. I had no idea how they got there, and Mom wasn't admitting a thing.

As Ruth's paranoia increased, this note, written on the back of a grandchild's photo, was often taped to her door at The Heritage while she was out for an activity.

Mom was progressively less involved in the food and activity committees, though she still attended most events. Her most important activity was dancing on Mondays and Thursdays with her gentleman friend, Jerry, a fellow resident. That never changed during her time at The Heritage. Twice a week Jerry carefully removed and folded his cardigan sweater, walkers were put aside, and the two glided across the floor. Age seemed to disappear as they danced every dance in the hour the music played. No one dared to cut in, as Mom was not about to share her partner. Her mind was clear about that.

The next big clue that there was a problem brewing came in the middle of Wells Fargo Bank. Mom said she had lost her checkbook and asked me to take her to the bank to get some spending money. You can imagine my surprise when instead of letting us withdraw spending money they told me she was $450 overdrawn with a list of charges from insufficient funds. Apparently, letters sent had been ignored. When I told her of the lack of funds, she was outraged and embarrassed. With hands on hips she said, "Well if that's how this bank does business, I'm just going to pull out all of my money and move it elsewhere." Totally taken off guard, I worked out the problem with an understanding bank manager. We would balance the account, and I would destroy any checks I could find. Later, in Mom's desk, along with the checks, I found other bills and pieces of business she had not addressed. It was obvious Mom was unable to handle even her limited finances any longer.

That day as we left the bank, a tired looking fellow with a ponytail held the door open for us. Having already forgotten the money incident, Mom said, "Well how nice to have a gentleman hold the door for us, and such a handsome fellow too. Don't you think, Bon?" Well what could I do but smile and agree? This was just the kind of thing she had embarrassed me with when I was younger. Now I was beginning to see the value in it. Ruth had worked her charm again. The man stood up straighter and a smile came over his face, apparently given a badly needed boost. He seemed less weary than he had been minutes earlier. She was generous with compliments. She wasn't thinking correctly about business at this time in her life, but she was still kind to others.

Life continued to spiral downward. The hoarding began. Mom soon had drawers filled with napkins, placemats, newspapers, magazines, and Kleenex. Often, while she was at lunch, I went to her room and threw away bags full of paper. I couldn't do such things while she was present, and it felt a bit deceptive, but she didn't seem to notice if I took them in her absence.

It wasn't only paper that she collected. We all chuckled when at a family potluck Mom's contribution was a bag of sealed jams and jellies she had taken off the dining room tables at The Heritage. On the other hand, maybe that was carryover for her generation of survivors, those who lived through the Great Depression. I've seen other older people in restaurants saving uneaten jam packets from their plates, so maybe that wasn't Alzheimer's disease. Perhaps it was just about not letting food go to waste.

Then came the next step in an all-too-familiar pattern among the elderly. Mom caught a bad cold that quickly turned to pneumonia. She was hospitalized for a week and was more than happy to go home. Not one to give in to sickness, and too stubborn to use a cane, she would not admit feeling weak and unsteady. Less than a month later, she fell and broke her hip.

The second hospital stay was harder on her. She was restless and seemed unable to understand all that was going on. Later, the doctor told us that surgery can have an adverse effect on an older patient. The damage done to her body, the altered oxygen flow during surgery, the inability to heal—all could have quickly caused an increase in her dementia.

Obviously, our mother was not going to be able to live on her own any longer. She had already been changing; now we knew she would never be the same person she had been. The family decided she would live with my sister Shirley in Salem where she would be surrounded by loved ones and have caring supervision. Mom happily agreed, though I don't think she realized that it was intended to be a permanent move, and how different her life was going to be.

My sister Nancy and I cleaned Mom's fully packed apartment. I can't begin to tell you what we found. We dumped bags and bags of paper goods. There was spoiled food in the refrigerator, soiled tissues tucked in strange places—indescribable things untouchable without rubber gloves. It was a heartbreaking task. We were grateful our mother didn't realize what a mess she had left behind. We left the apartment with boxes of clothing, a few personal items, and a rolltop desk. We hoped the desk and family pictures would be enough to make Mom comfortable in the room Shirley was preparing in her home.

Thus began the years of our family's journey into the dreadful disease of Alzheimer's. The ensuing events were sometimes laughable, often poignant, and always close to the heart.

2 Kidnapped!

It is not easy to recognize that a person close to you has the beginnings of Alzheimer's disease, especially if no other family member has been so diagnosed. Unless watching for the early signs, most people miss them. Many books are available on the disease, but the average person will not pick up such a book until the actions and behaviors of a loved one have become questionable.

This is exactly how our family reacted to our mother. Slowly we realized there was something very wrong with how she was handling life. Questions arose but we had not confirmed our suspicions. Alzheimer's disease was not yet part of our conversations.

Even before the bout with pneumonia and the fall that broke her hip, Mom had been showing signs of confusion. During the stay in the hospital, she was at times agitated or incoherent. Even as her hip began to heal, it was obvious she could no longer stay alone in the assisted living apartment where she had lived for seven years. My sister Shirley had said repeatedly that she would consider it her privilege to take care of Mom when she got older. The time was upon us. Shirley had worked as a practical nurse and had been involved in home care for several years. She had a spare bedroom. Two of her daughters lived with her and could help her out. Mom's caseworker was able to arrange for subsistence to help with Mom's expenses. It all seemed to fit.

While she was in the hospital, we started talking with Mom about moving out of The Heritage. She seemed happy at the thought of living with Shirley. We talked about Shirley's house in Salem, and what kind of room Mom would like to have there. She said she wanted lots of flowers and color on the walls. Mom liked bright colors. Shirley followed up by painting the walls a soft yellow with flowers and grass on the bottom half. The top was light blue with birds and butterflies. It turned out light and pretty. The room was furnished with a bookcase and Mom's rolltop desk. Family pictures were arranged for her to see. There was a calendar and a chalkboard so that they could talk about the day and time, hoping to keep Mom's mind current. Everyone wanted her to feel connected, comfortable, and secure. Before the move, family members sorted through her clothing. We picked out the outfits we knew she liked and hung them in the closet of her new room.

The biggest responsibility was going to be on Shirley's shoulders. I lived closest to Salem, but still forty minutes away in Sherwood. Nancy was in Bend, Oregon; Marge in Billings, Montana; and Russell in Hermiston, Oregon. I was still working a forty-hour week with Fridays off. We were all willing to help, but no one was near at hand.

When the hospital release day came, Shirley arranged to have Mom brought to her house. It was quite the event. Mom arrived in an ambulance. She had on a hospital gown, was being given an IV, and had no idea why her hip hurt. She was oblivious to what was happening to her. On arrival, she told Shirley she had been as quiet as a mouse in "that truck she had been riding in." When asked why, she said, "Two weird men kidnapped me and brought me here, and just look at how I'm dressed!" It was obvious that the kidnapping didn't bother her nearly as much as how she looked. That was our Mom, bless her heart. All of her daughters understood that part of her personality. Shirley found a dress that Mom liked, and clothed her properly. Little did we know that that dress would become an obsession for Mom. She wanted to wear it every day after that, not seeing it as stained or soiled. It was her security. But on that first day, at that moment, it seemed like the right choice. For Mom, the truck and the two weird men were gone. She was dressed and content to be in her new home, seemingly ready for the great challenge ahead.

Shirley and Ruth enjoying a moment together.

3 Getting Around

Shirley's house was full of women. Four generations lived together under one roof. Shirley's daughter, Deanna, was with her while she looked for work and a new place to live. Another daughter, Sherry, and her daughter lived in the basement apartment. They lived together as a family but each with their own schedules and lives. Mom was happy seeing everyone, but at the same time became confused by the coming and going. When I visited, she told me, "This place is like Grand Central Station," not realizing these people were all members of her family.

Mom knew Deanna, yet in the beginning of her stay, she didn't consistently recognize Deanna as her granddaughter. Shirley relayed to me a point of real contention that came unexpectedly when Deanna used Shirley's car. For reasons unknown, Mom thought the car was hers. Mom had given up her car and driver's license years earlier. It had not appeared to be traumatic for her at the time. Riding the bus had become her preferred mode of transportation. Why she was suddenly obsessed with the car was a mystery. When Deanna left the house, Mom would ask her, "When will you be back with my car?" Many times Shirley and her insistent mother waited up for "that girl" to bring back her car.

Shirley tried using logic and even showed Mom the title to the car—to no avail. Mom agreed with what she was told, and then five minutes later asked again, "Where is that girl with my car?"

We had yet to learn there is no point in arguing with a person who has Alzheimer's. You will not "win," and the person will become upset and agitated. Go along with what he or she is thinking, and life will be easier for all parties involved. A simple answer of, "She'll be back soon," is what Mom needed to hear. Not that it ended there, but it satisfied her for the moment. Mom even talked about how she paid for that car, the insurance, and repairs to keep it going, so no one else should be driving it. Somehow, she knew what it took to maintain a car, but she could not understand it was not hers.

Diversion was another tactic. When Mom started to get upset about the car, Shirley reminded her that she had given her car to her grandson, Otto, whom she loved dearly. Hearing his name, Mom forgot about the car and asked if Otto was going to come for a visit soon. Whatever the method used to distract her, it was still necessary to keep the keys out of sight because Mom might want to go outside and check on the car. It was hard to tell what she had in her mind. She often spoke about the drive *she* had taken us on, though she had not been the driver.

On another day she would ask, "I stopped driving a long time ago, didn't I?" Shirley would answer, "Yes, Mom, and Otto was blessed with your car." She liked that answer, and we all liked those days better—much less frustrating. Shirley showed a great deal of patience with the car ordeal. I doubt I could have done it at that point in Mom's care.

At first, getting around the house was a bit of a challenge for Mom, as she hadn't accepted the idea that she needed a walker. She made no connection to the fact that not using it was what had caused her to fall and break her hip. Shirley constantly watched to make sure Mom didn't take off across the room on her own. Another fall would have been disastrous. Mom's favorite color was red, so when Nancy and Marge went to buy the walker, they bought a red one thinking Mom would like it better. She acknowledged it, but that didn't mean she liked it! Mom thought walkers were for old ladies, not her. She told anyone who asked that she was sixty-eight. Must have been one of her "very good years."

With Shirley's help, wanting to or not, Mom mastered using the walker on the stairs and uneven sidewalks. If that was what it took to be mobile, that was what our determined Mom did. We all appreciated her wonderful spirit of independence. She challenged herself to overcome the increasing difficulties she faced.

Short walks eventually became long walks. Mom was happy with Shirley's neighborhood. She had a smile and a hello to everyone she met. My sister used this to her advantage by taking the opportunity to explain to neighbors that Mom should not be out of the gated yard by herself. "Because of her hip, she should never walk alone." We were all grateful that our mother lived in a neighborhood of watchful and caring people. Even with that, she seemed to feel most secure in the enclosed yard, but we could never assume she would stay there.

Later we learned the Alzheimer's Association can direct people to a program that encourages identification bracelets, necklaces, or pins—a good idea for folks who might wander. It is amazing how quickly a person with a walker can disappear. Leaving nothing to chance, bolt locks were installed high on the doors in Shirley's house where Mom seemed not to notice them.

Ruth's morning visitor, Queen Claudet. Q.C.'s
wake up routine delighted Ruth.

4 Good Morning!

Our mother was typically an early riser. I remember waking up to Mom singing in the kitchen. She liked to have her favorite country music station playing as she started her day. She would say, "Why have a bad morning? Nothing bad has happened to you yet." She once wrote a poem for Shirley which began, "Early morning I love best // While the world is still at rest." Even at this stage of her illness, morning was her best time of day. Her thoughts were clearer. Never mind that the night before Shirley might have been her friend from grade school and our mother was asking her what they would wear to school the next day.

Most often Mom reported how well she had slept the night before though family members had heard her wandering in her room opening and closing her dresser and closet at all hours. None of us wanted to get stronger sleeping medication for her because we wanted her thoughts to be as clear as possible. The problem was how to hold on to our mother's mind while our sister's became clouded from lack of sleep.

Shirley's family came up with a wonderful wake-up call. It all started when Shirley and Mom went to the pound to find a dog to keep them company. Pets are a positive influence on the elderly, but really, the family's reason for getting one was more that they just wanted a dog!

As the story is told—and it's hard to know about these things—either they picked this little white dog or she picked them. Either way, Queen Cluadet, or QC, as they called her, was the white, wire-haired Jack Russell terrier that went home with them that day. It didn't take long for a bond to grow within the whole family.

The morning routine became a joy. As soon as Shirley got up, QC left her bedroom and went into Mom's room. She jumped up on the bed, got the blanket in her mouth, and started pulling. When Mom awoke and knew QC was there, she drew the covers back over her head. The dog then pulled the blankets back again, carefully uncovering Mom's smiling face. It was a playful greeting, and QC's reward was a kind voice and gentle pat on the head. Mom told her granddaughter, Deanna, "QC tells me when it's time to get up. She comes in to see that I'm okay." They were such good friends. Though Mom remembered where they got QC, she often could not remember the dog's name. QC didn't mind. She just loved the gentle touches and the softness of Mom's voice when she spoke to her.

Deanna treasured her own morning routine with her grandmother as well. Shirley told me how Mom would sit at the kitchen table with her coffee as Deanna walked through the dining room barely awake. Mom would say in her perky little voice "Good morning. How are you?" To that, Deanna sleepily replied, "I don't know. I haven't had my coffee yet." This went on for a few mornings. Then one morning after the "Good morning. How are you?" Mom didn't give Deanna a chance to answer. In that same singsong voice Mom continued, "I know, you haven't had your coffee yet." Deanna had to stop to give her a hug. It was sweet having a loving grandmother living right there in the same house.

Shirley told us often that these moments of love were what fed the souls of that household while Mom was with them. Love was what she had to give. Her recent past and the present were almost gone; the future could not be faced or questioned. Her love was not held back, and it seemed to be expressed to each loved one unconditionally, even that little white dog, QC.

From Mom's Journal:

*Life is made up of little bits of
time and each is a gift for us to
love and cherish.*

—J. Carie Sexton

5 Incontinence I

No one in the family envied Shirley's job. Taking care of toilet habits with Mom was a twenty-four-hour-a-day task. Mom hid any items used for protection from incontinence. And when I say hide, I mean *hide*. Shirley said they were often torn to bits and stuffed in drawers, under pillows, in her jewelry box—anywhere. Nancy and I had seen this same activity when we cleaned out Mom's room at The Heritage. Still not realizing that Mom was heading toward Alzheimer's disease, I guess we thought some of this would resolve when her physical health improved. We couldn't imagine what was going through Mom's head as she denied everything about the incontinence. Was it pride, embarrassment, shame? I don't know. But it was a big problem.

Shirley began to feel a failure at keeping Mom and her room free from the smell of urine. She thought that when Mom came to live with her, she would give her regular showers and time her trips to the bathroom, enabling a schedule that would avoid accidents. Even Shirley's previous experience with the care of the elderly had not prepared her for dilemmas our mother continued to present her.

If the floor was wet, "The dog did it."

With the next incident, "Someone must have spilled water."

We needed to do something to help Shirley, so we had a family workday. The men replaced the carpet in Mom's bedroom with easily mopped linoleum. We all pitched in and bought a shampooer that worked well on furniture. At least it made the housework a little easier.

Shirley was challenged daily to get Mom out of her day clothing and into a nightgown. Mom preferred to wear her slip for sleeping, but everything smelled like urine by the end of the day. Shirley pretended to accidentally drop soiled clothes into the water because Mom wanted to put the same ones back on. Yes, it was still the dress she wore on the first day of living with Shirley. Mom would have worn it twenty-four hours a day. Even visiting family noticed, wondering if she needed more clothes. One day I took it home to repair (again) and just tossed it into the garbage. Mom forgot about it when she didn't see it anymore.

Though Mom's attitude was usually positive, days when Mom was uncooperative were physically exhausting for my sister. Mom was heavy and Shirley had an injured shoulder. Getting her in and out of the shower was the hardest. Mom tried to avoid the water stream and her balance was not good, so she often leaned heavily on Shirley. With other family living in the house, some chores could be shared, but Shirley handled all the hygiene issues.

Nancy and Russell came in from out of town to visit and encourage. I tried to get down to Salem on Fridays after my workweek. Marge came as often as she could from Montana. Mom loved the visits, and we had some days with good conversations, however the visits provided only short reprieves for Shirley. Mom frequently expressed her appreciation for Shirley and said that she had a great cook who was taking good care of her. Shirley accepted the praise gratefully but was finding it harder to stay on top of it all. Though Mom's hip had healed well, mentally she was losing ground.

6 Diagnosis/Acceptance

Shirley was beginning to feel more overwhelmed than expected. She needed to know what the situation was with Mom and if she was going to get any stronger mentally. Though none of the others in the family felt it necessary at that point, Shirley decided to inquire about an evaluation for Alzheimer's disease on Mom's next doctor's visit. By this time, Mom had been seeing a doctor in Salem for her hip, so Alzheimer's testing could be scheduled easily.

Most of us thought Mom would return to her normal bright and able self under Shirley's good care and close supervision of her medications. I can only speak for myself, of course, but when Shirley continued to suggest Alzheimer's disease, inside I kept saying *no*. From Mom's behavior, there obviously was some dementia. I thought perhaps she had taken excess medication over the years and it was taking its toll on her brain. We had no Alzheimer's in our family. Our grandfather had lived to ninety-nine years old and was sharp as a tack. Besides, Mom was not "the type" to get such a disease. She read a lot. She had been as socially active as possible at The Heritage. Mom was the first one the social directors called for an activity because they knew she would come. She participated in the exercise class, bingo, and lawn bowling. She especially loved dancing and the country rides the facility often provided on Sunday afternoons, when they might visit a llama farm, see the fall colors on nearby hillsides, or maybe just take a trip to a local store. Anytime a family member had a place to go, Mom was ready to join in.

Still following her instincts, Shirley spoke with the doctor. After describing Mom's behavior and her recent health history, there was no question in the doctor's mind that an evaluation was in order. Mom's doctor in Salem was wonderful. He was kind and thoughtful in his approach. He asked Mom a few questions about the seasons, simply judging her awareness of time, date, and place. Shirley said the hardest part for Mom seemed to be following instructions for simple tasks; she could not remember the order of the instructions. When Mom wasn't sure of an answer she looked to Shirley to respond, something she had recently begun doing. After just one visit with Mom, the doctor recommended a neurological physician. Further tests were necessary.

I still struggled with it all. It was not that I was sure Mom *didn't* have Alzheimer's disease, but I kept thinking, *So what? If she has it or doesn't, nothing really changes. She can't stay alone. Shirley wants her there with her. There is no cure. From what I hear they can only tell for sure after a person dies and has an autopsy. We are not going there. So why do we even have to keep talking about it? Life is hard enough for Mom now. Why do we have to upset her when it's most important for her to heal physically and become mobile again? We'll deal with her memory problems later.*

I guess I wanted to stay in denial.

At Shirley's request, Nancy and I went along on the next doctor's visit. We were impressed with the neurologist. He was attentive and sincerely interested in Mom's well-being. As Shirley had said, it was difficult to watch our usually sharp mother struggle to answer simple questions and be unable to remember the order of small tasks he asked of her. "Pick up the pencil, draw a box, then put down the pencil, and draw a circle with the pen." It was impossible for her. She could not remember the order of tasks. She didn't know what month of the year it was. We felt uncomfortable, uneasy. There was more lost than we had expected. The doctor proceeded with other common tests for Alzheimer's disease. He talked to her quietly and in a non-threatening manner. He asked her to do a drawing of a box inside a box. He had a clock and asked the time, about the seasons of the year, and who was our president. At that point she was beginning to tire and her response was, "Well you should know that without asking me!" Ever quick with an answer, I think she surprised the doctor with that one. With that, he felt he had enough to consider regarding her mental awareness.

Since then I have learned that we were fortunate to have such a kind, respectful doctor. Some doctors don't like to be bothered by elderly folks who are failing in mind and health. Some patients are dismissed to live out their lives as best they and their families can do. This seems to be the tragedy of the diagnosis: that he or she will not get better, only sink into the troubled world of dementia and despair. That was what our family hoped to avoid with our mother, but we had to face reality. With the evaluation came the fact that Mom did have Alzheimer's disease. Life was going to only get more difficult for her.

My reaction was, "Yeah, well, now what?"

The doctor explained there was no cure, but there was a medication, Aracept, that might help. It was the most current medication to slow the symptoms of Alzheimer's. It works on some patients but not on all affected. Hopefully, it would hold off the disease for a while and give us a few more years of enjoyment with our mother. Shirley went home with prescription in hand.

We hoped the medication would help, but only time would tell. To our relief, there seemed to be a difference in just a few days. Her hours of clearer thinking lasted longer.

Our mother stayed the same cheerful person she had been throughout her life. She appeared happy with all the attention she was getting. Her future was grim but she seemed unaware of where she was heading. I was all for keeping it that way. I still didn't want to say the "A-word" to her. Shirley felt we should tell her and talk to her about it so she would know what was happening to her thinking, that it might help Mom understand the frustration of not remembering a certain word or phrase or a person's name. Again my heart wanted to say, *So what? I have that problem too.* But my head was beginning to understand.

Would it have helped if we had recognized the symptoms earlier? If we could have started the medication sooner, would it have given her more years of clear thinking? I'm not sure. Each person and situation is different, but I believe early detection is the best choice. Keep an open mind.

With the diagnosis of Alzheimer's, Shirley felt she could go to the Alzheimer's Association to seek help and information. There was so much to learn. They connected her with a support group, which I recommend to anyone connected with an Alzheimer's sufferer. They suggested we take care of all legal matters that had not been resolved previously.

We began to talk about the realities of it all. It was necessary to talk about Advanced Medical Directives and Power of Attorney. I cannot stress how important it is to take care of this as soon as you realize what is going on with your loved one. We wondered if Mom understood when we asked all those questions. *Do you want life support systems? If so, how long? Who do you want to make that decision?*

I cringed when Mom looked at me after that one and said clearly, "I'll let you decide about that." *Oh great, they all heard her say that to me. I can't get out of it.* My mouth said what my heart didn't want to say, "I can do that for you, Mom." Power of Attorney was given to Nancy as she had assumed care of Mom's meager savings and bookwork associated with it. Truly, the whole process didn't take long, and I don't think Mom was bothered by it nearly as much as her children were. These were not threatening questions to her. It was a relief to have it done. All she had to say about it was, "Can we have lunch now?"

At this point I had finally accepted Mom's fate. Our mother had Alzheimer's disease. I didn't have to say it aloud but I knew it. I accepted it and tried to prepare for what was ahead of us. No use in denying it or being devastated by it. Each family member dealt with it in his or her own way. I decided to take it the way Mom would have in years past. I began to read and learn, gathering information. I can accept better what I understand. Knowledge is the key to being able to cope and survive.

On days when Mom could describe what *it* was used for, and could draw a picture and tell Shirley everything about how to use *it* but couldn't for the life of her remember the word *scarf*, they began to learn to laugh and shake their heads. What a mystery this crazy life had become.

Looking at this disease called Alzheimer's, I think the most important part of it for family members is acceptance— respectful acceptance of the person involved and acceptance of an irreversible situation. It was not an easy lesson for some of us.

We knew the beginning. We had talked about the end. Now all we had to do was figure out how to live out the middle of this unexpected journey.

From Mom's Journal:

Put some water in a cup and ask, Is this cup half full or half empty? The answer usually is—it's both. Yes, it is both. No one cup of life is full and no one is empty. Each of us has some happiness and some sorrow. A life is sad or happy depending on how one sees the cup—sorrowing always that it is half empty or rejoicing that it is half full. To this day when I am tempted to bewail my lot, I remember that a cup is half full or half empty. Then I see my blessings in proportion to my troubles.

7 Passing the Days

Each day, Shirley learned something new about our mom, about Alzheimer's disease, and about herself. At times Mom was right on target with who she was and who her friends and family were, other times not so. We could only accept and love her each day. Outside help made it easier for Shirley, including the Alzheimer's Association support group. Virginia Bell and David Troxel wrote an incredible book called *The Best Friends Approach to Alzheimer's Care*, which Shirley kept close by for encouragement and insight. The questions about this disease are endless. The medical field and caregivers alike seek answers every day.

One piece of great information gained from the support group was that there was a daycare program Mom could attend for one or two afternoons a week. It was sponsored in part by the Alzheimer's Association, and we were required to pay a small fee. It turned out to be a great resource. At first Mom was not sure she wanted to attend. She wanted her regular routine and was beginning to want Shirley to be with her at all times. Shirley insisted she try the daycare (which is when she started calling Shirley *The Boss*). With time, she looked forward to her group and soon began to think she was the person in charge of *the kids* at these gatherings. They visited, had a snack, and did many arts and crafts. Mom painted faces on nearly every project she did, perhaps because she loved people.

The hallway into the building held books and folders. Mom gathered each one going in and then again coming out. Shirley had quite the collection of information about the facility, the city, and even the state of Oregon.

Having the group keep Mom busy for just a few hours a week gave Shirley time for grocery shopping, running errands, or just taking a much-needed nap.

Deanna's artistic abilities were proved helpful in creating happy days for Mom, whose love of flowers and colors didn't change with the onset of Alzheimer's. Now Mom took the time to relax with a coloring book or colored paper and pencils to do an art project. Deanna brought out the best in her in that department. They kept themselves occupied for hours.

We all knew Mom had artistic talent, but she couldn't sit still long enough to do anything with it. While her sister usually carried something to knit or crochet, which she tried to get Mom to learn, Mom would say, "I'd rather be outside."

Mom could write a quick poem or sketch a chair or flower vase with little or no effort. It must have been something that came easily to her so she didn't see value in it. But now the offer of time spent with a coloring book was one she welcomed. Mom waited eagerly as Deanna laid supplies on the table, from which her grandmother could choose. Mom especially liked doing her "work" outside on the picnic table where she enjoyed the fresh air. She delighted in watching the antics of bushy gray squirrels in the large maple trees shading the back yard. She gave each one a name, often referring to them as rabbits.

During the evenings, Shirley played the piano for Mom and they sang hymns and old favorites together. Many times Mom gestured toward the piano and said, "Play something for me." They both loved to sing; it was so relaxing for them. It became a special part of their day.

In hindsight, that summer and fall was a peaceful interlude that wouldn't happen again. It gave Shirley's family memories to cherish and carry them through hard times ahead that no one could even imagine on those warm, happy days.

From Mom's Journal:

The busy have no time for tears.
—Byron

8 Letter from Deanna

Some time after Mom had moved to the Avamere in Sherwood, I received a long letter from my niece, Deanna, who now had an apartment of her own. I think she just wanted to let me know how much she treasured the memories she had of her grandmother and that she wanted those memories to stay with her—unchanged.

Dear Aunt Bonnie,

These are some memories I cherish and some of the reasons I found my grandmother dear:

She was kind. When I was young, she would set me up on the counter to tie my shoes so we could talk at eye level. She cut my pb&j sandwiches in quarters saying, "I made them small because you are small." Her unconditional love helped me learn the world has nice people, and it is okay to trust. She made me feel special.

Once I asked Grandma if she ever got angry with people. She said to me "Through the years I've learned that getting even with someone when I was angry never worked for me. It hurt me more than it hurt the other person. I just feel better when I'm kind."

She was bubbly. To me that meant bright, happy, cheerful, and a pleasure to be around.

I loved doing crafts with her.

She was beautiful to me. She looked younger than any of the other grandmothers in her pink coat and her blue sneakers. She put cold cream on her face every day. I still have some of those cold cream jars I secretly kept to hold rubber bands, household nuts and screws, and one for my own face cream.

I have mixed feelings about visiting Grandma at Avamere. When I tagged along with you and Mom, Grandma was concerned, saying, "Who is that girl?" It hurts me to see Grandma apprehensive and uncomfortable. Maybe it would be better if I went another time alone and she just accepted me as a kind stranger visiting her home.

Aunt Bonnie, I am blessed to have the rich heritage I have. I am proud to be Ruth's granddaughter.

Love, Deanna

Swedish Lullaby

Late one evening Mom and Shirley watched a movie together, which was not something Mom often enjoyed. However, this entire film was spoken with Swedish accents. Mom seemed entranced. When morning came, Shirley was greeted with *God morgon!* Our mom was greeting Shirley in Swedish! All our lives Mom said she had forgotten her first language, though she spoke limited English until she started school. The movie had triggered something in her brain.

For two blessed weeks after seeing the movie, Mom sang songs and spoke almost entirely in Swedish. Shirley loved it, and was grateful that some of the family got the chance to experience this special time with her.

Shirley said it reminded her of listening to our grandmother, who often began a sentence or conversation in English and finished it in Swedish. As a child, Shirley understood much of the language but could speak few Swedish words. I think there was only one phrase I remembered. *Älskling litten spädbarn.* It sounded like *stucka lila barn* to me, and I thought it meant *darling little baby*. It was the phrase Nancy and I used when anyone asked if we could speak Swedish—probably because it had *barn* in it, tomboys that we were. Our family regrets not learning more of our heritage, but at that time in history many immigrants were trying hard to be Americanized rather than holding onto old traditions.

Through Mom, Shirley heard again those songs of her childhood, which our grandmother had sung—a great joy and personal blessing to hear them sung in the Swedish voice of long ago, a precious gift in a small window of time that closed too quickly.

From Mom's Journal:

> *Those who wish to sing will always find a song.*
> —Swedish proverb

10 Family Christmas

Christmas time at Shirley's house began early in December with decorations and a Santa's Fireplace. Mom was excited about the holiday, and Shirley was thrilled to be spending it with her. It was an adjustment for Mom as it was her first Christmas away from The Heritage and her friend Jerry. She still talked about going *downstairs* which is where all the social activities happened at the assisted living facility. She missed her favorite dance partner and thought she needed a new party dress to dance in. Shirley knew she could get the dress and hoped that a family party would satisfy her expectant mother.

Shopping with Mom those days was interesting, to say the least. She paid little or no attention to size. Color was important—red being the most important. Trying on clothing was difficult, so Mom and Shirley picked items, knowing it was necessary for Shirley to hold onto the receipt in case they had to be returned. As Mom pushed the cart in front of her, using it as a walker, she pulled things off the rack and threw them into the cart, regardless of size. Because of her wholesale shopping style, Goodwill became the store of choice. Shirley let Mom shop for a while, then as Mom went on to the next rack, Shirley discreetly pulled items out of the cart and returned them to the previous rack. This trick became invaluable to the rest of the family when we took Mom shopping. Mom never noticed. Items that might fit, or that she might wear, stayed in

Ruth loved the Christmas decorations on Shirley's fireplace, but the memory faded faster than the Christmas lights.

the basket. Others were quietly pulled out. She didn't ask about the articles after the shopping trip. For Mom, the fun was in the outing rather than what she brought home.

One such shopping experience produced two pretty dresses that Mom thought were perfect for dancing. Christmas was coming near and she was ready.

Mom helped Shirley as much as she could with the tree decorations for the Christmas Eve and Christmas Day celebrations. From her chair in the dining room, Mom supervised the preparations.

There were family gatherings and big meals followed by gift opening. It was a warm and wonderful holiday. At least that was what everyone else thought.

When it was time to take down the ornaments and the tree, Mom wanted to know when we would have Christmas. Shirley said her heart sank. It was as if Mom had missed the whole thing! Had nothing registered in her mind? Had all the people and commotion been more than Mom could absorb?

The bad thing was, Mom did not remember the dresses, the food, or the fun. The good thing was, she forgot that she didn't get to dance. We can guess her personal happiness came in experiencing moments during the celebration. There appeared to be no memories for Mom to recapture, but her presence made it a Christmas Shirley will treasure forever.

11 Transition

Home care might be the first choice for a person with Alzheimer's disease, but it is a difficult task for the caregiver.

Our mother's easy personality made the job doable for a time. She was generally a happy person. She ate well and, for the most part, was cooperative. For Shirley, the hardest part was having to be alert to problems twenty-four hours a day, at night being in that half-asleep mode in case Mom got up and turned on the water or the gas stove. Shirley felt unable to leave Mom alone in the house or the car for even a moment in case she became disoriented and panicked.

In a home, there are still chores to be done, meals to cook, and the general running of a household. Toileting problems and extra laundry add to that. Caregiver fatigue becomes a huge factor. What often happens is that, in time, the caregiver grows so exhausted that he or she becomes ill. Meanwhile, the Alzheimer sufferer continues at their same health level even as they seem to require less sleep.

A good mantra might be: *The Alzheimer's patient is only as safe and healthy as the caregiver in charge.*

This also means there might be some temporary unhappiness within the Alzheimer's patient or within other members of a family if the person has to transition from home care to facility care unwillingly. Each caregiver needs to be honest about the situation and their own abilities to care for another human being no matter how much they love that person.

Thank goodness we didn't have that problem. We were all on the same page, but nonetheless, this is where we found ourselves—in transition. Shirley could no longer care for our mother. Shirley's health was suffering, she was moving, and her life was increasingly complicated. It had been a blessing for Mom to be with her, but the day had come, as we all knew it would. She needed to move on.

But, how? Who? When? And especially, where?

We had to find a place for Mom that would provide twenty-four-hour care. Though none of us wanted to do this, there was no choice. Looking back, we realized Mom did thrive at the assisted living facility, moving there of her own volition. If she were making this choice, she would most likely again pick community living over foster care in a private home.

Guilt is a worthless emotion in these instances. But how do you shed it? It clouds judgment and keep us awake at night. We needed to put it aside and make a logical intelligent decision about Mom's future.

Life is never constant. We must accept change. We must transition.

The task of finding the full-care facility fell to me. It was unfamiliar territory for me and I didn't particularly want the responsibility, but I knew I needed to do it for Mom. I hadn't felt like the daughter closest to her, but now I wanted her to be where I could regularly watch over her care. As it often is in other cultures, it looked as if the youngest daughter's duty would be to care for her parent. I wasn't sure I was capable of this new role, but I knew I would learn.

I found an Alzheimer's care facility close to my home. Working full time, I needed a place that would be convenient for me. Avamere at Sherwood had just opened and they were accepting Medicare residents. I had looked at several other establishments, and only one other took Medicare. Regardless, I liked Avamere. It had short hallways painted a soft yellow. There were pictures of dogs and flowers on the walls at an easy eye level. A great fenced-in courtyard outside the unit had a circle walkway allowing residents to be outside safely. I took Mom to look it over. Her first comment was, "This is a beautiful place. I could live here."

My prayers have been answered, I thought gratefully. I had been concerned that the transition from home family care to a care facility was going to be difficult. I was relieved that Mom felt good vibes from this place.

My sister Nancy and I visited the facility when they hosted an open house, and we felt good about it. It was close by and seemed to be a good fit. The decision was made.

The day we moved Mom, my sister Marge came from Montana for moral support. Nancy was there from Bend, and her son Otto came to encourage us on an emotional day. Though Shirley knew the move was necessary, she felt it would be too traumatic for her to face. She chose to stay away. I'm sure Mom didn't know exactly what was going on but sensed it was something important. She showed her inner strength. She was calm and seemed content to stay in this "new hotel," as she called it.

We were all apprehensive, but Mom's transition was in full gear.

12 Locked in Memories

A week after we moved Mom into The Arbor, the locked Alzheimer's unit at Avamere in Sherwood, I stopped in to see how she was adjusting. The staff had suggested we make just a few short visits for the first month, as it might be upsetting for Mom to see us coming and going. She needed to settle in, they said. It was hard to stay away, and yet it was a relief to leave as well.

She had questions that day. "How long will I be staying here? It's a nice place but shouldn't I be going home? Are people looking for me?" It was hard to know the right answers. I wished I knew what to say. I was going to have to get better at this. I left The Arbor feeling heavy with a huge lump in my throat.

Avamere's staff had warned that some of the new residents might try to leave with me. I carefully closed the door behind me, being sure it latched. I heard clearly the distinctive click of the door lock. My independent mother was locked inside. Suddenly and unexpectedly, tears filled my eyes. The last month had been a nightmare for me. There had been floods of emotion that I kept hidden in an imaginary box to be opened later or not at all. I went to my car and wept, trying to let go of the guilt I couldn't shed even though I knew it was unwarranted.

Mom's formal diagnosis months earlier had left us all wondering what was ahead for her and for us. We were grateful that she had been able to stay with Shirley for a year. Shirley's home was generally a happy place for Mom but it was a busy household. The people-traffic began to confuse Mom as she forgot the faces and the connections with some family members. One niece who was also living with Shirley had nightmares and often called out during the night. This triggered Mom's mothering instinct, and soon she was up turning on gas burners and rattling pans in preparation of a formula of some sort to quiet the grown child. During the day, she often walked out the door to look for her car, or for some other unknown destination. My sister was surprised to see how quickly Mom could move when no one was watching.

The year of care Shirley had given our mother had taken a toll on her own health. Her damaged shoulder ached everyday as she struggled with our resistant mother in the shower and when getting her dressed. The lack of sleep and the emotional ups and downs were causing her blood sugars to run rampant—not a good situation for a diabetic.

We all knew this was the right thing to do, but even after finding this place, I was still uncomfortable with what felt like locking up my mother. I needed further assurance. My oldest son reminded me, "Gram said she didn't want to live with any of her children when she got older. And remember how excited she was to move into The Heritage Assisted Living? She chose to live there, Mom. This new place will be like that."

I called my daughter in Indianapolis. Her comments were, "You're creating a safe environment for her. Mom, you're experiencing your own feelings of fear of confinement, not hers." My daughter knows me well. She was right; I do have an issue with confinement.

That conversation brought back a childhood memory that was part of what I was feeling. I was eight years old. My mother, her friend Lucille, Lucille's five-year-old son Russell, and I were going to San Diego. We were going to attend the Naval boot camp graduation of Lucille's other son, Evan. As was typical of my mother, the straightest route to anywhere south went through Reno, Nevada. She was not a high roller by any means—it was just a change of pace for her—but we joked that she needed to buy a round-trip fare when she went to Reno for a holiday.

We pulled into Reno late that night. I remember walking up the narrow stairs in what was probably a seedy downtown hotel. Even at eight years old, I was uncomfortable there but had no clue why. Russell and I were immediately put to bed. The two women relaxed for just enough time to think that we were sound asleep. Then they left us. The door lock clicked with certainty. I haven't forgotten that sound and the feeling of helplessness. *What if Russell wakes up and starts crying for his mother? What if the place starts on fire? We can't get out. What can I do?* The door was locked. The clamor of drunken arguments and the constant movement of people coming and going in the hallways were frightening to me. Maybe because I was the youngest in the family, I was used to having someone else in charge. A sibling was with me constantly. I was relieved Mom and Lucille were not gone long, but it felt like an eternity to me.

I look at that memory as just a moment in time and place and circumstance. But that locked door is still with me. And now here I am locking doors on Mom.

I believe she knew the doors were locked at Avamere, though she called it *the doorbell.* When she did ask I assured her, "We want you to be safe. No one can come in and bother you." I used the words I wished she had said to the eight-year-old girl in Reno, telling her that the door was locked to keep her safe, not to trap her inside a scary place. Strange which memories from childhood stay with us.

People with Alzheimer's disease are often like that frightened child. They need to be in a safe and secure setting. They cannot be expected to use good judgment. The time comes when a twenty-four-hour care facility is the surest way to protect their health and well-being. They need to be in a place where they need never be frightened. The locked door becomes their security. I must let go of the guilt.

13 Incontinence II

There we stood in a daunting aisle of enormous packages of incontinence products. Oh yes, I had heard all the Depends stories. I'd read all the funny birthday cards alluding to the use of such things. But somehow I hadn't expected so many brands, styles, and shapes, or even sizes. They are different for men and women, but that's the easy part—in fact, the *only* easy part.

In the beginning, back in Mom's early stages of Alzheimer's disease, we were in denial of many things. When we cleaned out her apartment as she moved to my sister's house, we found some strange things in Mom's garbage that looked like shredded toilet paper. We couldn't figure out what they were or why such things should be found. Later at Shirley's house the incontinence problem became more evident. Shirley repeatedly shampooed her carpets and furniture. Mom wouldn't actually admit having a problem. I don't know if she didn't recognize it or if she was too proud to accept the problem. She did, however, get frustrated with the cleanup. Shirley had to get creative in getting Mom to change her clothes.

When Mom moved to the Alzheimer's unit of an assisted living facility we were all ready to see how the pros handled it. I'd like to say they got it right and all was good after that. Nope. They ran into their own problems with Mom.

Unfortunately, the incontinence products provided by the facility were not at all acceptable to my mother. For one thing, they were bulky. She was still concerned with appearance, and she thought they made her look fat. She preferred to wear dresses and "those things" were not flattering. We all got that message loud and clear. The staff put them on her, and she took them off. The big difficulty in that is that she took them off and hid them. Or she might take them off in someone else's room and leave them there to be found later. She even took them off in the restroom of a restaurant when the group went out for lunch. On such occasions, the activity director had no knowledge of the situation until a wet bus seat or telltale wet clothing was spotted. Oops! Too late!

Mom and many of the other residents did not like to be told when to go to the bathroom. They resented being treated like children even though they were not responding to natural urges.

One caregiver in particular figured out ways to get around Mom's obstinate behavior. Instead of saying it was time to go to the bathroom she said, "Ruthie, it's time to freshen up your lipstick. We'd better take care of that in case you have company." Now that was important. Mom followed her to the bathroom with no argument.

When accidents happened, odor from the urine-soaked pads and clothing was strong. Showers were necessary, but I'm sure all residents felt a certain vulnerability in their nakedness. When it was time for that morning ritual she hated, Mom had to be coaxed into the water with a song and dance routine—literally. I was told the song was usually "You are My Sunshine" and the "partner" danced Mom into the shower with little effort. If the caregiver stayed close by, the water running over her head was not as threatening, but she disliked having her hair washed.

Naturally, these tricks didn't work every time. I heard about mornings when Mom's walker was thrown against the wall and words came out of her mouth that no one was accustomed to hearing from her. I'm thankful that I was not there to experience those days. When I expressed sympathy regarding those situations, the caregiver said, "Don't worry about it. At least we know she still has spunk." I am grateful there are caregivers like this one who took time to really know Mom's personality. Such caregivers are a blessing to the residents and their families.

Even with all they were able to do for Mom, it was still necessary to replace the carpet in her room with a tile floor, just as my sister had done when Mom stayed at her house.

One day, while on a doctor's visit, the nurse asked Mom to remove her clothing and put on a gown. We saw she had no underwear on to remove. The nurse looked at me and I looked at Mom, dumbfounded. When I questioned Mom her response was, "I left them in my room. I don't need them!" Before we left, the understanding nurse scrambled to find something we could put on Mom to get her home dry.

After a good chuckle about my bare-bottomed mother, the caregivers and I devised a plan. They would do a subtle check before Mom left on an outing. The caregiver would put an arm around her waist as if to give Mom a little hug and then let a hand slide down on Mom's hip, checking for the bulkiness of the pad. Mom didn't catch on to that. But I had learned my lesson. I would not be caught like that again. I carried extra Depends in the car.

That's what brought us to the store to buy incontinence products. My sister and I chose three different kinds. All were different from those Mom disliked so much at the facility. I left a few with her in her room. We tried the different styles to see which one caused the least resistance. Some were way too bulky. I couldn't get the ones with Velcro to stay up. The pull-up type seemed to work best. I had a few at my house in case Mom had an accident. Really, it wasn't even an "if." It was a "when." Neither Mom nor I was comfortable with toileting. She still wanted to be independent, and I wanted her to be. However, as time progressed she couldn't make it in time or make it all the way onto the toilet. I waited outside the door until she called, then helped her stand up to put dry pull-ups on her, all without talking about the problem. She would say, "Oh these are so much better than those things *they* put on me." I liked them because they didn't leak and they were easier for me. No matter what I used at my house, I knew I would be scrubbing the floor after her visits. It was just part of the deal.

Naturally, this was a common problem for many of the Alzheimer's folks. Family members shared situations at support group meetings in order to learn from one another. That's where I learned to carry a large towel to put on the seat of the car using the hot sun as a reason to have Mom sit on it. Other people had different solutions.

On one occasion, I heard a fellow say he was planning to take his mother on a ride to the beach the next day. Remembering earlier discussion of his mother's incontinence problems, one person asked, "Didn't you just get a new car? How are you going to manage to keep it from getting wet or stained?

He smiled and said, "Oh I'm renting a car."

From Mom's Journal:

Blessed are they who understand my faltering step and palsied hand.

Blessed are they who know today my ears must strain to catch what they say.

Blessed are they who seem to know that my eyes are dim and wits are slow.

Blessed are they who looked away when coffee spilled at the table today.

Blessed are they with a cheery smile, who stop to chat for a little while.

Blessed are they who never say "you've told that story twice today."

Blessed are they who know the ways to bring back memories of yesterdays.

Blessed are they who make it known that I am loved, respected, and not alone.

Blessed are they who know I'm at a loss to find the strength to carry the cross.

Blessed are they who ease the days on my journey home in loving ways.

— Ester Mary Walker

14 Jerry

One of the heartbreaking consequences of Mom's going to live with Shirley after her fall was the loss of her relationship with her good friend Jerry. The Heritage Assisted Living Facility where Mom had lived and where Jerry currently lived was in Tualatin, an hour away from Salem. It was not easy to coordinate busy schedules with the time commitment required to get them together. Jerry called her, and that helped, but the telephone had become confusing for Mom at times. Often she didn't understand why she couldn't see her friend. Things had changed drastically since they first met.

I remember groaning when my sister told me Mom had a new "boyfriend" at The Heritage, where she had been living for several months. We had all been a little puzzled by the move and, frankly, it didn't feel right. Was she actually admitting to getting old? No, that wasn't like her. In that respect, I should have been happy to hear she had found a boyfriend. At least I knew she was still connected with life. As in the past, she needed to have someone to take care of and someone to make her feel special. I had not been particularly fond of her last male friend, so I was not anxious to meet this one. What a pleasant surprise to meet Jerry. He was articulate and nicely dressed. Much like Mother, he was interested in current events. He also considered himself a golf aficionado.

Ruth and her favorite dance partner, Jerry, enjoying activities at The Heritage.

Jerry was a huge part of Mom's life over the next months and years. When we couldn't reach her by phone, we knew we could catch her at Jerry's apartment. They sat at the same dining table and were regularly involved in lively conversation about world events. They spent Sunday mornings together reading the newspaper and watched golf tournaments together on the weekends. Mom hadn't been a golf fan, but she knew that one way to a man's heart was to take his interests as her own. Soon she knew the names of all the great players and could tell us anything we might want to know about Tiger Woods, Jerry's favorite.

On Tuesdays and Thursdays Mom and Jerry were first to arrive for the dance music. Both dressed appropriately for the date. Jerry's favorite cardigans were a soft yellow one and a red one—worn in part because Mom liked it, I'm sure. Mom wore one of her flowing dresses, often a gift from Jerry. Oh yes, and without fail, Chanel #5 perfume, also a gift from Jerry. Walkers were put aside and cardigan sweaters folded neatly on a chair. They never missed a dance, and the regular musicians knew them on a first-name basis. They made time to play Mom and Jerry's favorite, "Somewhere, My Love." It was a pleasure to see them on the dance floor. Years melted away from their bodies and minds as they flowed together with the music, Jerry's slim form guiding Mom smoothly across the floor. As I watched them I wondered how different Mom's life would have been if they had met earlier in their lives. About dancing Jerry would often say, "I don't understand young people today. Why do they want to dance separately? Half the fun of dancing is holding your partner close." He had such a twinkle in his eye. He took pride in his ninety years. Rather than thinking it was the end of his life, he seemed to see it as a time to have fun. Unfortunately, Jerry fell and broke his hip one day while they were dancing. He had a hip replacement and recuperated well, but there would be no more dancing. They both missed it. It had been the highlight of their week.

In the evenings they got together in Jerry's room for a nightcap. He had an affinity for Wild Turkey whiskey. Not in excess, mind you, just one drink each evening to help him get a good night's sleep, not enough to interfere with medications. I heard tales from the staff about my mother walking down the hall to Jerry's room with her little tray of attractively arranged crackers and cheese or a decorative bowl of assorted nuts to accompany the nightcap. She might even be wearing a brightly colored muumuu with a flower in her hair.

Our family and Jerry's applauded the relationship. Mom and Jerry had a wonderful time together. The fun they shared gave meaning to their lives. Most of their family members worked and couldn't spend much time with them during the week, but that didn't matter because they had each other. Jerry had a weekly game of bridge that he never missed. Mom was a little more interested in the field trips offered by The Heritage and did those without Jerry. Most other activities found them both participating.

They also went on outings with both families. Jerry's family was accepting of Mom, and we loved Jerry. He used to like to come to our house for barbecues. He was a slight man, but he could put away an amazing pile of ribs. It was fun for us to cook for them; both were so appreciative. If we slacked off for a while Jerry would say, "Boy, it must be about time for Jim to barbecue again soon, isn't it?"

Jerry was a sharp guy. He could carry on an interesting conversation and loved to tell tales of his younger days on the golf course or of his dealings as a car salesman. He could quote interest rates and deals as if they were done yesterday. Later, even as Mom's conversation became increasingly repetitive, Jerry was patient with her and continued to keep her on track.

Their contented lifestyle soon came to an end.

By the time we moved Mom from Shirley's house to Avamere, it was almost too late for the visits, but we made it work for a while. It all became a ritual. Jerry would call me either Saturday evening or early Sunday morning. He'd ask if I were going to bring Ruth over to visit. He needed to know so he could bring up some dessert or fruit from the kitchen. He took some childish pleasure in sneaking food to his room. I would tell him that we would be there about two o'clock in the afternoon.

I'd pick up Mom and we would go to The Heritage. Many people there remembered her, but she found it increasingly difficult to remember them. She might say to me, "I used to live here didn't I? I wish I could still be here." I would tell her that they didn't have any rooms left there so she would have to stay at Avamere. I told her I would keep my ears open for a spot for her. As time went on, she would say the halls were too long for her so she might be better staying where she was at now. I happily agreed.

As we moved down the hallway towards Jerry's room, he would be waiting. (Heaven forbid we be late!) Sometimes he would hear us coming and would peek around the corner and wave at us. It was touching to see the happiness in this man's face when he saw Mom.

So there we were, but logistics were not easy. Both of them had walkers. They had to maneuver the legs around in order to give each other a kiss. Like clockwork, Jerry told Mom how nice she looked and how happy he was to see her. She glowed under his compliments. Then we would move into the apartment. Mom had trouble getting up from Jerry's couch so he kept an extra pillow on the couch for her. There would be a small table all set up with a china plate bearing an assortment of cookies, candy, or fruit—all arranged carefully—as well as three cups and saucers. A carafe would be on the counter of his kitchenette area. It was my job to take the carafe down two floors to the kitchen and fill it with fresh coffee. As I left on my errand, he often commented that I could take my time in case he wanted to steal another kiss. When I returned I poured a cup for each of us, then we visited about whatever was happening in the news or sports. We were expected to eat everything he had for us. After a half-hour of pleasant conversation, I left them alone for an hour and went to the grocery store for my weekly groceries. Within a few minutes of my return Mom and I would leave. It was the same scenario of tangled walkers to enable good-bye kisses. Jerry would tell me to bring Ruth back next week, and off we'd go. He watched us leave, often with tears in his eyes. He truly missed her company.

That was our routine for a few months, but the situation became more difficult. Mom had befriended another resident at Avamere. Sam was a pleasant man, younger than Mom. She started referring to him as "Jerry." When we actually saw Jerry, she would say how old he looked.

Because of the denied incontinence, we were battling the Depends during this time. On a couple of occasions, the cushion at Jerry's was wet when Mom got up. And Mom didn't like the long walk from the car to Jerry's apartment. She began to get restless when the conversation got too complicated for her. The visits were obviously not as enjoyable for her as they had been in the past. Though Jerry kept calling to see if we were coming, Mom no longer seemed to care about going. She had transferred her attention to Sam and now didn't know the difference.

I felt bad for Jerry. I knew his health was failing and now his heart was broken. They had been so good for each other. Together they had been a couple everyone at The Heritage knew. Separately they were just two old people facing ever-shrinking lives. At least Mom had someone else to spend time with but Jerry never had another special friend. About a year later, I saw his obituary in the paper. The funeral had already taken place so I didn't get to go and say goodbye to this kind gentleman. I was grateful for the friendship he had given my mother during her stay at The Heritage. They had found the wonderful gift of companionship that not everyone finds at their ages. I'm sure they both had a special place in their hearts for one another. He has certainly held a tender spot in mine.

From Mom's Journal:

If you have love, you have everything. If you don't have love, no matter what else you have is not enough.

15 Reluctant Student of Medicine

L uckily, there has been little need in my immediate family for involvement in the medical world. Medications, medical processes, and even medical dramas on television hadn't been of much interest to me. Conversely, my mother felt the medical field was something to be admired and held in the highest esteem. She would have loved it if all of us girls had followed her into hospital work. Mom had enjoyed her work in the hospitals but that sentiment was lost on three of her four daughters. Only her third child, Shirley, would become a nurse and caretaker in her professional life. Thank goodness one of us went in the direction Mom had hoped for. Consequently, Shirley was referred to as *the nurse* in the family. She was the one to whom each of us, especially Mom, directed our medical questions, and I was glad to have it that way. I took some light personal abuse on that subject more than once. At one clinic visit Mom asked a medical question of me, and my response was an honest, "I don't know."

"Why not?" she challenged.

"Because I'm not a nurse," I answered.

"Boy, you sure aren't!" she responded with more than a little disgust in her voice.

After Mom stopped driving (and long before Alzheimer's), my role in medical care was to be one of those who drove her to doctor appointments and to pick up her medicines. A day at the clinic for Mom was like a day at the park for the rest of us. She looked forward to it and to all the attention she got. She dressed appropriately. It was predictable that Mom would wear *nurse white* on doctor days. I'm sure she was often the most pleasant patient of the day. She carried her list of medications as if it were a certificate of merit. She knew what prescriptions she was taking and why. It seemed to me that she took more medication than necessary, but I rarely said anything and most often didn't really pay attention. I was just there to chauffeur. I had my own full-time job.

When she started running out of some medications early, it became a bit of irritation to me because it created a need for another trip to the clinic. It should have been a clue, but I was oblivious to any other problem at that point. I thought a simple scolding from the doctor was going to straighten her out. Not so.

While she was living at The Heritage, I tried several times to convince her to purchase her meds by mail, but she made all kinds of excuses and said it just didn't work right. I knew it worked because I was ordering my one prescription by mail with no problem. Time would tell us that many things were not working for Mom at that point. When she started showing other signs of confusion and forgetfulness regarding medications, the family decided we had to start watching more closely. Was she overdosing herself? In fact, we figured out she was forgetting whether she had taken the meds and so took more. When she took them at the wrong time of day, it played havoc with her blood pressure. The pill organizer didn't help. If the sleeping pills didn't work fast enough, she took more. Mom thought she ran out early because they didn't count right at the pharmacy or someone might be stealing her pills—another unrecognized early sign of Alzheimer's-related paranoia. After a family consultation, responsibility for ordering and dispersing medications was turned over entirely to the caregivers at the assisted living facility. That seemed to solve the problem. But somehow, old prescriptions showed up in her medicine cabinet occasionally. We didn't know where else she might have medications tucked away, so we frequently checked her room. It was best to do that while she was in the dining room or at an activity. Mom was independent and didn't appreciate being spied on. However, if we did throw various meds away, she never seemed to notice or ask where they had gone.

Shirley reviewed Mom's medications while Mom lived with her. Once again, the *family nurse* had addressed the problem. I stayed in my semi-avoidance mode. With Mom's diagnosis of Alzheimer's and the doctor's prescription of the new medication Aracept, Shirley stayed in charge, and I kept the basket over my head.

Now I know better. It is important to stay abreast of new information. Early detection and early treatment can make a difference. At first my attitude was, *If she's got it, she's got it. There's nothing we can do about it. Let's just make the best of it.* I now see that was wrong. With early detection, the person suffering from Alzheimer's can help make decisions as to how they want to live out their life. It gives them the chance to take care of personal business. Here the personality of the person and how far the disease has progressed is so important. To some, diagnosis can be an incentive to do things; to others it might be a blow too discouraging to face. Each family needs to decide. In the end, I was glad Mom was diagnosed. We understood her actions and behaviors better and could begin the medication, but it still wasn't something I felt we had to remind her of each day. She knew she was having a problem. There was already so much for her to deal with.

A year after her diagnosis Mom came to Sherwood to live at The Arbor, the special care Alzheimer's unit of Avamere

Assisted Living. I assumed responsibility for the overview of Mom's care and medication program. I didn't know one pill from another and really didn't want to know. I was ready to hand over all the medicine stuff to the in-house nurse and the caregivers there, but it just doesn't work that way. I had to be involved. I found that sooner, rather than later, family members should become familiar with what is going on with the health of their loved one—even in a care facility. I was finally dealing with her mental health, but I needed to become aware of what else was going on with her body. There was definitely a steep learning curve for me.

Though most caregivers are conscientious and good at what they do, it is important to be personally familiar with the meds lists and schedules that are set up for your loved one. Healthcare facilities often have high employee turnover rates. Shift changes, telephone calls, and multiple distractions can cause a caregiver to forget to write down important information regarding medications. *You* are the constant. Take notice if there is a difference in attitude, sleepiness, or agitation that may be caused by pain. Sometimes Mom could tell me if she wasn't feeling good, but other days it was, "I'm just fine," when she obviously wasn't. Even watching how she got up from a chair or walked could provide a clue. These are the things you become aware of that you might not have noticed in earlier days. Talk to the caregivers about what you see. Share your concerns. It helps them do a better job.

The doctors' visits now came with many questions directed to me. Mom was happy to answer the questions, but her information was cloudy and unreliable. When asked, Mom said she had no idea why I had taken her in that day. "I feel great!" she said, as she limped in favoring her left hip. When asked about medications, she said she didn't take any, as I handed over the long list provided by the caregiver. Still, there was value in her participation in her healthcare. She enjoyed the interchange and needed to feel she was involved.

Mom was happiest when the doctors were men. If the doctor were a woman, Mom would ask, "Are you sure she's the doctor, not a nurse?"

I would say, "Yes, I'm sure," and she would ask, "Are there any men here? Is she the only doctor in the place?"

"Yes, Mom."

Disappointed, she would concede, "Just my luck. Well, she must be pretty smart then."

I had to remember that in her generation the majority of doctors were men, so I think she had more confidence in them, as well as still hoping for some male attention.

I didn't feel knowledgeable about all those medicines and long medical terms, but I was good at asking questions. Mom had bouts of gout, which were terribly painful, and her medications needed to be increased to deal with the discomfort. I'd ask, "Should she have a cold pack on her wrist to help reduce swelling?" Her legs would swell and water pills would be increased to control the fluid retention. "Shouldn't her legs be elevated? Where are the *ted hose* we ordered for her?" For those of you, like I was, who are not familiar with them, *ted hose* is the short name for those tight elastic socks that are worn to help blood circulation. Usually white, there are several different kinds and lengths. They need to be prescribed by a doctor. They were a nagging problem for Mom. She didn't want to wear them, so she hid them. If brown ones were shipped to her, it was even more likely she would "lose" them. She hated "those ugly brown things!"

I did not feel intrusive asking questions of the caregivers and looking at med schedules. Mom's arthritis would flare up and again pain meds would be increased. "Did you start (or stop) the medications? Has the nurse visited her? Is it time for a doctor's visit to make adjustments?" These were all things I tried to keep an eye on when I visited. My mom was not one to complain about how she felt, so I had to take the advocate role for her. A caregiver can get to know your loved one, but you can recognize signs that may not be obvious to a newcomer. Help them out, but realize criticism can cause hard feelings. If you feel an issue has not been resolved, make a point to talk to the health nurse or the facility administrator.

At one point, Mom became quieter and seemed to be depressed. We discussed the situation at the next Care Conference, which, by the way, should include the facility administrator, a caregiver, and, if possible, the nurse. The others had also noticed a change in Mom's disposition. After a doctor's consultation, an antidepressant was added to her meds. It was a small dose but it seemed to improve her attitude.

In a discussion at a support group meeting, there were those who thought antidepressants were not appropriate. I knew my mother, and I wanted her to have a feeling of well-being. I didn't want her over-medicated, but I had missed her smile and her talk of "getting a job in this place." We all missed her participation in her already too-small world. The medication helped her enjoy life more and helped her sleep better— important factors. Again, each family has to make their own decision on these matters after discussing it with staff and doctor to ensure what is appropriate.

We have a history of diabetes in our family. Mom began showing higher blood sugar levels. Family history, her age, inactivity, medications, and diet were most likely all factors to her borderline diabetes. She was put on a low-sugar diabetic diet and her food intake was monitored. Monitoring, in Mom's case, meant limiting high-sugar dessert or too much of the wrong starchy foods. Naturally, those were often the foods she loved, which caused some disagreements.

I was sometimes the culprit in boosting her sugar levels by showing up with a strawberry milkshake, and Mom was still able to charm a tablemate out of his dessert from time to time. I learned that when I took Mom out for lunch or to my house for the afternoon, I needed to tell the caregivers what she had eaten so they could adjust the next meal or at least expect the higher sugar levels. Working together we were able to avoid having to add any diabetic medications.

As the Alzheimer's disease progresses, medications still need to be reviewed on a regular basis. *Is there a point where it makes less sense to continue with hormone or cholesterol medication? Should the pain medications be given later in the evening or maybe during the night to ensure a better night's sleep?* These are not your decisions to make, but they are good questions. Don't be afraid to ask. Be the advocate.

Before the Alzheimer's journey ends, you may end up knowing more than you ever wanted to know about medications but knowledge answers concerns, and with it comes more peace of mind. You need that.

A successful day of fishing for Ruth. Look at that smile!

16 Patriotic Fishermen

It was a gorgeous day to go fishing. There is nothing like September in Oregon when the sun is shining. The temperature was perfect and the sky was as blue as it could possibly get. The group going fishing at the Sandy Trout Farm was from the Avamere Assisted Living facility. There were a few folks from the Alzheimer's unit of the facility, including my mom. This was the most well-groomed, spacious, fishing farm I had ever seen. The paths were easy to navigate and the ponds were accessible and well stocked. All were ingredients for a great day.

As a volunteer, I was to help put worms on the hooks, cast if necessary, and assist when needed to land the fish. One amazing thing about the old folks is that they remember how to do things they liked to do in the past. Even from wheelchairs, some were able to get their lines in the water. The smiles on most faces were as bright as the sun overhead. But one lady started crying. When I asked her what was wrong, she said it just made her think of her father and how much he had loved to fish. There was no comforting her, as she was lost in her recollection. Some shook their heads and said no, they didn't want to fish, but their eyes told another story. When I handed them a pole not one refused. Others who had gone fishing often, like my mom, got so excited when they saw the fish coming out of the water.

Each person was allowed to catch two rainbow trout, and they were beauties. The activity director laughed saying, "Oh dear, I think I've gone way over my spending limit in fish for today." Of course that brought on talk about limits and firsts and biggest fish. Were these the same people who had gotten off the bus earlier looking old and tired? I'm not so sure. They had forgotten about the aches and pains of life but remembered the right fishing lingo and the competition of the sport. It was fun to watch the transformation.

As the fish were being cleaned, we moved the group to the eating area and started to set up food for the picnic. When the fish were delivered, we put a little butter, salt, and pepper in them and foil wrapped each one for the grill. One woman stepped up and asked if she could help. She said she and her husband had run a small restaurant locally and she missed the work. She was a great resource and enjoyed every minute of it. Others helped set tables. It took awhile to get the fish done, but every person was willing to wait, and each had their fill. I have to say, those were some of the best trout I've tasted.

After a wonderful dessert of chocolate cake, we cleaned off the tables and packed things for the trip home. As I picked up paper plates I said to Mom, "Isn't this a wonderful place to be today?" As if cued in an onstage musical, she started singing "God Bless America." I was taken off guard at first but soon joined her song. As I had been thinking of the small space of the trout farm being wonderful, this marvelous lady was thinking of *America* as a wonderful place to be. I was so proud of her at that moment.

One by one, the whole group joined the singing, some putting their hands over their hearts. The realization came to me that we are losing this generation of incredibly loyal Americans who sacrificed more than many in other generations will ever understand. What a wonderful heritage they have given us.

Even though Alzheimer's disease and age have taken so much from these folks, they still remember their patriotism. The moment brought tears to my eyes.

Then came the topper to this wonderful day of fishing and food. It was a comment from one of the fellows as we headed for the bus. He said, "Boy, we sure know how to have fun don't we?"

17 A Letter Never Sent

Hello to each of you,

Since it's close to Mother's Day, I thought I might write this letter to all of you to help you understand how our mother is right now. It might also help you have a more satisfying visit when you do come to see her. It is a hard place to go to, and I know we all agree that this is certainly not what we wanted for Mom.

I hear complaints about conditions at the care facility: Mom doesn't smell good; Mom's not clean; the food looks awful. *The fact is, the staff is overworked and trying their best, but it's still not always good. They tell me they are constantly interviewing because they can't keep enough help. If you see something you don't like, say something to them, or ask to speak to the administrator. It would reinforce the requests I have already made.*

That's not really the point of this letter, though. Let me give you a few suggestions about visiting. For starters, don't go there around a mealtime. That is a very structured and important part of Mom's day. Shirley can verify that. If it's time to eat, she's going to eat whether you are there or not. She will get up and walk away from you when food is served. As you might remember, that was the case before she ever left The Heritage. In reality, that is how it has to be.

For the best opportunity to see the Mom you used to know, take her out of the facility to visit. She still loves a car ride. She likes to see the flowers that are blooming right now. She often asks, "Where have animals gone?" She gets a big kick out of seeing the llamas at the farm just outside of Scholls, or seeing ponies or pigs. It doesn't have to be a long drive. She's okay with an hour or so. A trip to Shari's for lemon pie and coffee is something easy that Mom enjoys. She will talk more and interchange more when she can be one to one. Remember, some days are better than others for her, but that does not mean she doesn't enjoy the visit. I've had her at my house when other people were there. She'll be real quiet and seem out of it all, but when I take her back to the facility, she'll say, "That was such a nice day for me." She still likes having company and being with people.

But take warning. Before you take her out, be sure to ask one of the workers to check to see that Mom is "dry." I've had so much conversation with them about this that they should not even question your request, and they will do it discreetly. It's embarrassing for all and uncomfortable to have accidents— much more so than the small discomfort you may feel in having to ask. I was in a hurry when I went to get her on Easter Sunday. The caregivers knew I was coming, so I assumed she would be ready. I brought her to the house only to find she had nothing on under her dress and she peed all over my floor. She had probably stashed the Depends in her room somewhere, but it was not her fault. It was mine, for not making sure before we left the facility.

There will be times when you come to take Mom out and you'll have to change her dress if the one she has on is not clean. This, too, is nothing new. It was happening before she left the Heritage. How many times did she have to change our clothes and clean us up when we were children? We've just reversed roles now. Just remember, you cannot be in a big hurry to get going when taking Mom out. It doesn't pay. I've had to stop running everything to the last minute where she is concerned. A change for me, as you all know.

Speaking of that, the short "stop in" for fifteen minutes doesn't always work so well either. I've tried that on my way home from work, but it accomplishes little more than confusing Mom. It might take her that long to connect, even though she knows you are family.

Mom has been in Sherwood for a year now. She does some pretty bizarre stuff down there from time to time. These last couple weeks have been hard for me, as a lot of things have come up. (Mom got into a hassle and slapped another lady over a purse, for one thing.) I try to work through the problems with the administration and/or the nurse. Since I am still working, it puts more pressure on my time and life. It's not as if they aren't taking care of her needs, but I still feel a big responsibility to make sure her life is as pleasant as it can be now. So I guess I'm repeating myself, but... She does remember family and friends even if she doesn't know their names, and she does love an outing. I know it's difficult when you're not close by, but suggest to your families here that they help in that way. The day will come when she doesn't know or care anymore, but that is not here yet. Remind them that if it's been a long time between visits, she may need a moment to recognize them—but give her that chance. It would be nice to have someone else take her out to get a haircut or to eat Chinese food. I'm sure she would enjoy different visitors.

Every Sunday morning at 7:30, Jerry calls me to see if we're going to come to The Heritage that afternoon. They both enjoy those afternoons so much, I find it hard to say no to his request. What else do they have? She seems to come back to more of the old norm when she's there with him. It feels like an important connection for her, but a fragile one that might easily be lost if not continued. Don't get me wrong. It pleases me to see her and Jerry visiting, and I know I have choices as to how I spend my time, but watching out for her welfare is a responsibility I take pretty seriously.

It makes me smile when I hear her singing every word of the Hank Williams CD at my house. I wish you all could have seen her face light up when she heard "Nikolina" on the Scandinavian tape Marge sent to her. There are great moments to be experienced here, and I'm taking them all into my heart.

Anyway, back to Mother's Day: If you want to get something for Mom, I have some suggestions. She needs bras and slips. Hers are worn out and sometimes disappear— don't ask; I don't know where they go. Many of her dresses are too small for her now. She has gained weight with no exercise and the prednisone medication she's on for her breathing. If you could pick out something nice for her at a Goodwill or secondhand shop near you, it would be great. Mom seems to have lost interest in going shopping with me, though she still likes getting new things. She tells me it's too much work to go, but you could ask. She might go with you.

She usually needs bath powder and, as always, red lipstick is still a necessary item. She likes flowers in her room. They need not be fancy. Daffodils in a mayo jar would work. She still likes to read, so any magazines, old or new, will be appreciated. On some evenings, she will read to the group. I think we should encourage her in that as much as possible. She still wants the Sunday paper, though I'm not sure how much she gets out of it.

Don't send money to her, that concept is gone.

Hope I'm not sounding like the whining sister, but I needed to get it all off my chest. Please come when you can. Mom still needs your love and attention.

Love to all,

Bonnie

This is a letter I wrote to my family one day while feeling frustrated and angry with the whole situation, but it was put in a drawer and never sent.

18 It's Off to Work I Go

The day came when I realized I was running out of energy. When we moved Mom to Avamere in Sherwood, I thought I would easily handle all of what was ahead. After all, the facility was in charge of her daily care. All I had to do was get her to doctors' appointments and stop in to visit her on a regular basis. I would keep up the Sunday visits to Jerry and get my grocery shopping done while they visited. All manageable, right? Well, apparently not so. Months had gone by and it wasn't getting any easier. I was often able to reschedule my work hours to accompany Mom on some of her outings, but it would create a pile of unfinished work to be done the next day. I felt guilty putting an extra load of daily tasks on fellow workers.

The company for which I worked had changed hands, and the new owner was a company located on the East Coast. The sale had caused a number of changes, not all to my liking, and it was stressing me out. I was getting weary of the daily grind, I guess. My husband was tired of me coming home and slamming the car door with such animosity. The ten-hour days and traffic made after-work visits to Mom more difficult than I had expected, as well as making dinner later than we liked. Many of my Fridays off were filled with Mom's medical appointments and evaluations as well as shopping for her personal items and/or taking her to a salon for a haircut. Saturdays were left to clean the house and take care of our regular yard work;

Sundays, church and then off to Jerry's. Seemed like little time for anything else. Life was not what I wanted it to be. Something had to change.

It was just Jim and I at home then, so Jim suggested I quit my job. He could see the toll my busy schedule was taking on me, but I wasn't sure I was ready to retire. At the same time, the new-owner situation made it sound appealing. I had expected to work four more years, but I had to reevaluate my priorities. I wasn't even sure what the new company had in mind for me. I didn't think a part-time position was possible given the workload. Timing is everything. I could continue working, but the time spent with Mom would have to decrease. I had no idea what was ahead for her. I thought, *Should I hope she hangs on until I can retire as planned, or do I retire early and enable a much more pleasurable time with Mom?* For twenty years I had worked as a purchasing agent and manager. I enjoyed the everyday contact with vendors and the manufacturing floor, but it was a high-stress job. Sudden schedule changes could put the buyer in difficult situations with little room for error. A buyer was either the hero or the villain to the sales department, depending on the scenario. My inner voice said, *Maybe it is time to let myself take the sentimental, less stressful choice.* To add to the picture, months earlier our daughter had had a premature baby who struggled to survive—another reminder of how unpredictable and fragile life can be. Making machinery simply didn't feel as important to me anymore. I gave a two-month notice to my employer.

I know this is not a choice everyone can make. I understand fully that every paycheck is necessary for many. Giving up mine did change some spending habits for us. I'm thankful my husband was instrumental in and supportive of my decision. It made life at home easier and gave me the time I needed to spend with my mother in her last years—but this action is not for everyone. Each of us has to make life choices that work for our families, without outside pressure or guilt.

I tried to use this precious time with Mom wisely, taking her home with me often, visiting her on other days, and taking part in the facility's activities. It was a blessing not to have to keep up with a forty-hour workweek as well.

As the Alzheimer's disease progressed, I seemed to use less time for Mom. She could no longer leave the facility, and as a result, her health problems seemed to become less volatile. As life's pressures and exposures diminish for Alzheimer's sufferers, there's a period wherein many actually experience an improvement in physical health, by default. Mom caught the colds and flu others in the facility had, but it required nothing of me, as the caregivers asked that we *not* visit during those little epidemics. Often one of the local doctors would come in on those occasions, and/or the health nurse would stay close to give flu shots or other medications.

Those were the times when I thought I could have made a different choice, possibly downgrading to part time, but still, I'm glad I made the one I did. Financially, it had a cost, but it has all worked out in the end.

I'm grateful that I was able to enjoy more time with my mother in her last years. Big decisions are not easy to make when someone you love is involved. I was lucky to be able to follow my heart.

19 On Volunteering

Caregiving, in the usual term, is not natural for me. I'm not so good at helping with baths, feeding, and the one-on-one personal stuff. So much has to be done. Even when your loved one is in a care facility, it can be overwhelming at times. Volunteering was my way to feel I was doing something to help Mom and the situation as a whole.

I volunteered to help at the Alzheimer's Association one day a week. They are happy to have a volunteer for one day, one morning or afternoon, and at special events in the area. They offer many valuable programs, and all need people power. They may need help on the phones, with the library, mailings, follow-up telephone calls, and—with some training—the hotline. The obvious benefit is that you can learn much about Alzheimer's disease in the time you spend in that environment.

For those not interested in the disease itself, volunteering could offer an opportunity to gain experience in general office work or provide a perfect setting to learn how a nonprofit organization functions. A volunteer could gain experience in operating a help line or even get a feel for 911 response. A call to your local chapter will present you with a myriad of opportunities to help a wonderful organization.

If your loved one is living in a care facility, volunteering to help on the field trips is a fun thing to do. Typically, I offered to meet the group at their destination rather than taking a seat on Avamere's bus. This enabled more folks to participate and allowed me to head directly home after the event if I had other errands. At first, I wasn't totally comfortable doing these activities, but after I got to know more people, it was fine. They just need you to be there, since some outings are not possible if there aren't enough volunteers assisting. The folks love the outings, and it is so good to keep their minds active and interested, and to witness their joy.

Another volunteering activity came about due to a passion I shared with Mom—a love of flowers. I seemed to accumulate flower baskets and didn't know what to do with them until I came upon an idea that served a dual purpose. I would make small flower arrangements in them—nothing complicated, and most often just flowers from my yard—and take them to the activity director at Avamere. She would use them for bingo prizes. Being able to play with my flowers and give some others a bit of color and freshness for their rooms was a boost for me as well. Mom thought she was getting special treatment when I brought a small vase of flowers just for her. Sometimes she wanted to share them; other times she wanted them put right into her room.

Help is generally needed for special barbecues and food events. Maybe your comfort level is making a great dessert or salad. The gift of food is welcomed, and it gives the facility residents a taste of something different than the everyday fare, no matter how good that might be. These folks do appreciate it. To be safe, ask the facility director to fill you in on their policies about bringing food from home.

I took advantage of Mom's birthday being in May by making strawberry shortcake for those in the Alzheimer's unit. It made Mom feel special and most people loved the fresh strawberries. It's important to arrange that your food gift coincides with snack time or lunch. Check with caregivers on this one, because they may need to make adjustments for those with diabetes.

When our apples or pears were ripe, I often sliced them into a bowl and took them to Avamere. Just offering them to each resident provided a sense of connection. There were thank yous and comments from some who otherwise seldom spoke. Living in a rural farm area as we do, many asked if we grew them ourselves and seemed pleased when I said they came from our orchard. Maybe it triggered something in their past and took them back to an old reality.

Sharing a collection of small statues of horses, dogs, or elephants can also bring back good memories and provide enjoyment. If you have something to share, talk with the activity director. They may have a time slot they would like to fill on their schedule of events. It's good to share things folks can hold comfortably in their hands, things that are not fragile or easily broken.

I took in my ten-piece horse statue collection. In contrast, another day a family member brought in her lipstick collection. Both were enjoyed. Other ideas might be the old-fashioned penny banks with movable parts, or something as simple as baseball caps or cards—especially if each has a story behind it. Sport trophies are another idea. It's surprising what will spark conversation. Be careful, though; as the residents sit in the circle and admire the objects, things can disappear into a pocket quite nimbly!

If there is no activity director, schedule time with the caregivers before you come in with your box of memories to share.

At times, the facility may have an event planned that you can help facilitate. Ask the caregivers how you might be able to help. They will give you suggestions, and you will feel good being able to do something useful that is within your comfort level.

I often joined the group activities, even if I wasn't personally sharing anything. It was so rewarding to see a face light up when an object like an old toy tractor suddenly struck a memory in an old gentleman, or a special song warmed the heart of a woman and she was able to sing along. Those are the moments that count as blessings. Moments that good are when family members need to be present to enjoy a time of clarity and happy thoughts.

Activities are important to the mental awareness and well-being of the Alzheimer's sufferer. Attend as often as you can, and help whenever you are able.

The blessings are many.

From Mom's Journal:

> *As you climb life's ladder,*
> *You can reach a hand below,*
> *Just to help another fellow*
> *Up another rung, you know.*
> *It may be that in the future,*
> *When you're growing weary too,*
> *You'll be glad to find someone*
> *Who will lend a hand to you.*

20 A is for Alzheimer's, Anxiety, and Annie

A nnie lived in the same Alzheimer's unit as my mother. Her loving and patient husband Dean lived on the assisted living side of the facility but would spend everyday with her in the "special unit." I did not know them before they came to stay at the Sherwood Avamere. They were quite the pair. She was petite, maybe all of ninety-five pounds soaking wet, and he was probably six feet two inches tall. They were in their late seventies. Their devotion to each other was obvious. She would say to me, "Isn't he just the cutest guy." I would tell her how lucky she was to have such a handsome man, and she would say, "Oh he's more than just handsome." Dean would sit and smile, enjoying the compliments. They were just fun to visit. I was touched one day when he said to me "We like you because you like us."

I had learned that she was a teacher in her working days. It made sense, as she often seemed to be trying to organize people, seeing that they were comfortable and that they had something to do. Of course, some of the residents did not want to be organized, but that was not her concern.

She would say things like, "Oh, your sweater just makes your outfit," or "That color is the perfect complement." She made the type of remarks my home economics teacher used to make. It made me smile.

One sultry day in August, the activity director asked for a volunteer to go to the county fair with her group. It consisted of some folks from the assisted living side and some from the Alzheimer's unit. I enjoyed going on outings with my mother, so I went along. I met the folks at the fairgrounds. On these outings, it felt good to be there when the bus arrived in order to help the folks get off the bus. Many would recognize me and say hello, and my Mom might say, "How did you find us here?" as if it were a stroke of luck.

We had lunch in the shaded area of the fairgrounds and then took a tour of the barns. Annie and Dean were right there with us. As the day got warmer and Annie started getting tired, you could see the distress in her eyes. She began to ask where the bus was and how we all would get home. As Mom's friend was pushing her in the wheelchair, I took Annie's hand and tried to comfort her. Dean reassured her as well but it was definitely getting to be an overly long day for her. At one point, she took my hand out of hers and put it in Dean's hand. "If you will just take care of him, I think I'll be okay," she said.

A short time later as the group headed for the gates and the activity director went for the bus, it was all I could do to keep Annie from panicking. It was too warm and she needed the comfort zone of the facility. Everything around us suddenly seemed threatening to her. I felt badly for the anxiety she was feeling. As the bus pulled up, we made sure she and Dean were among the first to board. Dean quietly tried to calm her, but her eyes still showed the fear and anxiety that Alzheimer's disease will bring. We learned that day that Annie would only be able to go along on shorter trips. This one had been too much for her. I told the group good-bye and patted Annie's hand as I left the bus. She took my hand and asked where she was going. I told her she would soon be home. With honest concern she said, "Oh thank you, but will you please pray for us to have a safe trip?" My heart melted.

"I most certainly will," I assured her. "Don't worry anymore today. God will get you home safely." It seemed to comfort her.

The next day I visited the unit again, and there were Annie and Dean, fully recovered from the excursion. I greeted them. She asked me if there was anything she could get for me. I assured her I was fine. Then she asked, "How do I know you?" I reminded her of the fair we had attended together the day before, not really thinking she would recall. She said, "Oh yes, and it was very hot."

I said yes, pleased that she had remembered.

She said, "You can see I still have a 'fair' memory." Her little face broke into a smile as she realized what a clever pun she had made. I couldn't resist giving her a hug. What does Alzheimer's disease do to the brain to let it work so well some days and other days it's all short circuits?

Annie is gone now. Her stay at Sherwood was only a short couple of months. She became ill and had to go to a nursing home where she passed away. Dean stayed at the facility for a while but was lonely without his partner of many years, so he went to live with one of their children. I miss seeing the two of them sitting together on the sofa, her chatting and organizing, him patting her hand and smiling lovingly at his soul mate.

21 Haircuts and Happy Times

Even though a person has been diagnosed with Alzheimer's disease, it is still important to have that person looking as good as possible. It makes them and you feel better. My mom was careful about her appearance. One of the most important things to her was that her hair looked nice and had color in it. (I might add she had some truly interesting colors in her day!)

One day when I picked her up from the care facility, she was in a rather confused state of mind. We got her hair cut and a nice color put in it. As she waited for me to get my hair cut, I noticed that her conversation had become more rational and alert. She was looking at the spot on her dress and trying to get it off. She saw the run in her sock. She was more concerned about her appearance than she had been earlier. She also talked about how good her hair felt and looked.

I brought her up to my house for supper after the appointment. The hairdresser and I had told her how nice she looked, but it wasn't until my husband complimented her on the great cut and color that she really began to glow. What other women said was okay, but she still loved those compliments from men. My husband had picked up on that and played right into her personality. I love him for it.

"Maybe we should go dancing tonight, as pretty as you look," he teased.

"Good idea," was her answer as he helped her out of the car.

Mom needed all the feel-good strokes she could get. She still wanted to feel attractive. The personality that was there before the disease struck was still in there.

I'd better warn you, though: this hairdresser thing can backfire. Our hairdresser, Teresa, didn't make the color dark enough one time, and did she hear about it! Mom may have not been able to tell you what day it was, but she knew her hair was not the color she had in her mind. Both the hairdresser and I got a tongue-lashing. Believe me, we wrote down that "right" color.

Our hairdresser got such a kick out of her. They had some good conversations. Mom had had three husbands and a few boyfriends in between. One memorable conversation about her husbands got confusing, and at one point I said to her, "My dad was Clarence." Her response was "Oh that's who I 'was with' when you were born." We all had tears of laughter in our eyes before she finished telling that story.

On a good day when I said we were getting her hair done, she'd ask if we were going to see that girl "in the back." She couldn't remember Teresa's name but still had an association with where she worked in the beauty shop. I'm sure it was the stimulating girl-talk that made the haircut outing more fun. A piece of lemon pie at a nearby restaurant added to the day.

As her disease progressed, it became too difficult to go outside the care facility to get Mom's hair done. There was a good hairdresser on site who was wonderful with the residents, but for as long as Mom could go out, I felt it important to make the hair appointment part of an outing for her. It was fun for both of us.

From Mom's Journal:

> *Just because you're good looking, you don't need to be seen all the time.*

22 A Christmas Past

Christmas 2001 was a bittersweet holiday for me. The Alzheimer's disease from which my eighty-five-year-old mother suffered made it a little confusing for her. In her own bewildered way she loved all the decorations and the singing that went on in the special unit of the Assisted Living facility where she lived. Many times she told me there were no celebrations at her facility, but by checking her activity schedule I could see there had been fun things for her to do. She had just forgotten.

I wanted to take Mom to a Christmas Eve service. Dinner was a little late in her unit that evening and a group of schoolkids was there singing, so she didn't want to go with me. I know it was nothing personal. She was enjoying the activity. It was too much trouble to get up and go out when she had the children's choir right in front of her, not understanding that they were almost at the end of the program. In her pre-Alzheimer's days, she would have had her coat on in a flash and raced me to the door.

I especially wanted her to go with me to church this year. I was beginning to feel uneasy about how little quality time I was going to have with Mom. I guess the holidays magnified my fear of losing her. *How much longer will she remember family traditions? How long will she really know what we're doing and why?* I wanted to dress her up in her red suit so everyone could tell her how nice she looked. Instead, she wore her practical, washable, blue patterned dress. I wanted to hear the Christmas story with her again. I knew she would love being in the church. I wanted her next to me singing all the old familiar carols, which she still followed word for word, note for note, without pause. I wondered if she would be able to do that next year. I knew I would truly miss hearing her sing.

During the holiday preparations, one thing took me by surprise when I brought her up to my house to help with the decorating—an activity she loved. I had purposely left the ten-piece nativity scene for her to unwrap and set out on a table. Since arranging and rearranging seemed important to her then, I thought I had picked the perfect project for her. It proved to be more difficult than I ever would have imagined. I showed her how to unwrap one piece from the tissue paper so she could see what we were doing, then left her there to finish while I peeled potatoes for dinner. As I watched her from the kitchen, I could see that she was confused. I explained again what we were doing. She grew quiet and carefully folded a piece of tissue, still not really knowing what to do next. I sat down beside her and handed her a piece to unwrap while I unwrapped one alongside her. It took well over twenty minutes of concentrated effort for her to get through the remaining seven pieces, and even then I found one piece, the baby Jesus, in the box still unwrapped. When we set the pieces out on the straw-covered table, she didn't seem to recognize the scene. Nor, did she mention Mary, Joseph, or Jesus by name. I wanted to cry. It seemed so sad. I had to realize that it had been a year since she had heard or talked about Bethlehem or the miracle of the baby born there. Much had happened to her in that year; much had been forgotten.

On Christmas Day Mom again puzzled me. She kept asking me about my new house. She wondered how long it took me to find it and if Jim, my husband, liked it there. She complimented the way I had decorated it. At first I couldn't figure out what she was thinking. Finally it dawned on me that she was confused because I had moved things around in the house. There was a tree in the living room and different things on the walls. Because the place looked so different to her, she thought we had moved to a new house. She even mentioned it to my brother later at dinner. In reality, she had visited us in this house for twenty-seven years.

Presents seemed to be fun for her, yet a bit of a mystery. The thoughtful caregivers from her facility had given her gifts. They said she cried when she opened them. I had gifts for her too, but because I had written only her name on them, Mom didn't know if she was giving them or getting them. She loved the candy. She opened it and sampled immediately. Likewise, she opened the bath powder. When she smelled how nice it was, she decided to put some on her face and all over the dark-colored dress she wore. Oh well, she was happy and she smelled great! I talked her out of opening the makeup kit I bought with money from her sister. She wondered why her sister would send her anything. She liked the nice warm gray cardigan my brother and his wife gave her. Instead of thinking of how stylish it was, I found myself thinking, *Good, it's washable,* and *Great, it has pockets for her lipstick,* not to mention the constant collecting of anything paper.

Later when my sister gave her the favorite Aplets & Cotlets fruit candies, Mom got a little teary eyed and said that Nancy had given her more than she ever deserved. It was a poignant moment for all of us. As she looked at the new picture of our sister Marge and her husband Howard she said, "What a nice picture. They look happy. They must love each other a lot." Where does that insight come from amidst all the other confusion?

It was comforting to see that food was still something Mom enjoyed. She looked for the things with zesty flavors like pickled beets or asparagus. We had to keep an eye on her though. It wasn't wise to leave the relish dish in front of her or even the jams and jellies because she might decide to have them as a main dish. Desserts were as popular with her as ever, and again we had to kindly and quietly monitor how much she partook. I should also add *quickly*, as her hands moved fast when she wanted one more piece of pumpkin cheesecake. Without fail, she expressed her thanks and appreciation for the meals. "I can't tell you when I've had such a good meal," she'd say. She often added, "I don't cook much for myself anymore," or "It's hard to cook for just one person." Of course, it gave me pleasure to cook for her and to make the food I knew she loved. After all, in the past she was the one who made my favorite macaroni and cheese for me when I would visit her alone because she knew my family didn't like it. We all remembered what a good cook she had been and how she loved to feed us.

We were pleased when our sister Shirley called to wish us all a Merry Christmas, but I couldn't be sure who Mom recognized on the phone and who she didn't. This day she did recall her second daughter and seemed comforted by hearing that Shirley was fine and having a good day. Her mothering instincts still kicked in, and we knew she wanted us all to be happy.

By five o'clock that afternoon, Mom was getting tired. When she saw that my brother was getting ready to leave, she asked if he would take her home. She must have felt safe and secure with Russell because Mom had become afraid of the dark—another recent development. I had taken her out for dinner a few days earlier and thought we would drive around town to see the beautiful Christmas lights. She was quite nervous. She thought we should have brought Jim with us in case anything happened. She said maybe I should stay overnight with her at Avamere and go home in the morning when it was light. She looked at the colorful lights fleetingly but commented that she hadn't been out much at night and thought that maybe we should head home. It was obvious that this was no longer the treat Mom had enjoyed in days gone by.

The big day came and went. Mom enjoyed much about it. I had to be reminded again that with Alzheimer's nothing stays the same. We have to pick out the easy things that work and let go of the expectations we carry because of our history with this person. We need to take comfort in the fact that *we* probably feel the biggest loss. Our loved ones don't usually realize what's been taken from them. All we can do is help them enjoy their moments and keep precious memories in the back of our minds for times when we need them desperately.

Happy New Year? You bet! Even with Alzheimer's disease, there was so much for Mom to appreciate and enjoy in the year to come.

23 Sundown Syndrome

It came slowly, and I didn't recognize it. With the shorter days of winter bringing early darkness, maybe it just became more noticeable.

When my sister Shirley commented that she didn't want Mom to become "institutionalized," I didn't really think there would be a problem. Mom was living in an assisted living facility then, but she was still mobile. What Shirley was referring to was letting a place or a schedule rule someone's life. You know, something like the woman who needs to get her shopping or appointments done before *General Hospital* comes on at three o'clock. Innocent enough.

But it did happen. The longer Mom lived at the assisted living facility with its defined hour for meals and its time for exercising and social hour in the piano room, the more apt she would be to say, "I think we'd better go back now. I think I forgot to sign out. They are going to wonder where I am." The other line was, "I think we've done enough today. It's time for lunch at home," meaning the facility. It was about habit, but it was also about comfort zone.

The more extreme of this behavior is called Sundown Syndrome. It's common in different degrees with the elderly. The first time I saw it was when Mom was admitted to the hospital with pneumonia before she was diagnosed with Alzheimer's.

What a wild ride that turned out to be. She seemed fine during the day, but as soon as the sun went down Mom grew disoriented. I went to the hospital from work one day to check on her progress. She and her roommate looked exhausted. I was told they had had a tough night. The other woman would just get to sleep and Mom would whip the curtains open, close them, and whip them open again.

I asked, "How are you doing?"

"I'm tired from being up all night hanging the curtains. Don't they look better now?"

The next day when I visited, Mom had been moved to a private room closer to the nurse's station so they could keep an eye on her.

The worst night was when she somehow managed to call me on the phone to beg me to come and get her out.

"They are being mean to me and tied me to a chair. I don't even know where I'm going to sleep tonight." She was crying. Thank goodness for my husband's common sense and logic in keeping me from going to the hospital to rescue her. Of course, there would have been little I could do for her. Her mind was racing out of control. I thought perhaps the medications were causing her to hallucinate.

She was released five days later, weaker but seemingly back to normal.

She wasn't quite steady on her feet, but even the brightly painted cane I bought for her in Mexico was not attractive enough to convince Mom she needed extra support. She fell and broke her hip, which required surgery and another hospital stay.

We went through much of the same process with the Sundown Syndrome. One night she thought I had black spots on my face and kept telling me to go wash them off. "Go look in the mirror," she insisted. I couldn't stay long because it was so upsetting for both of us. Another night she saw cars coming through the windows and was terrified. It was hard to watch her suffer through the illusions. There was no calming her. Yet during the day she seemed much better, more rational.

As we progressed further into Alzheimer's disease, we learned that when we took Mom out for any occasion we needed to be back *home* before dark. It wasn't so much disorientation now as it was fear of the dark, the unknown. Mom needed the comfort of her familiar environment after the sun went down. Sundown Syndrome now affected her life daily.

24 Miss Sticky Fingers

*W*ell *what do you know? Miss Sticky Fingers has surfaced again. She has followed my mother around for several years now, and this time Mom says I get to see her in action. Now she is living here at Avamere at Sherwood, and she is not even trying to hide.*

Mom hadn't put a name to her yet, but looking back, I remember when Mom was sure someone had stolen a pair of slacks she had laundered and hung on the line behind the duplex where she lived. She was relentless about the slacks disappearing. Despite looking high and low, we didn't find them, so maybe that was when the culprit began to plague Mother. I only doubted the theft because at the time, Mom would leave behind a sweater or a pair of shoes whenever she came to my house. This *forgetting* was happening quite often.

Shortly after that, Mom moved into The Heritage. That's when the problem came to the forefront. Clothing, jewelry, and small trinkets disappeared. We listened to all that Mom said and were naturally concerned. Care facilities sometimes have a reputation for things being stolen. Off to the administrator's office we went, calling foul play. New to all this, we were a little upset when they said there was not much they could do without proof.

Thanks to her friend Jerry, Mom accumulated more things. At the same time, more items seemed to be missing from

Mom's room. (Maybe this should be a lesson for all of us: If you have too much stuff to keep track of, you have too much stuff!)

At first Mom had no suspects, and then she zeroed in on one attendant. Mom had dubbed her "Miss Sticky Fingers" and was sure this woman was jealous of all the gifts she was getting. Mom wanted it stopped. To the office we went again. But still no proof, no motive. The woman Mom suspected had no history of doing any unscrupulous deeds. The administrator was understanding but could do little to confirm or calm Mom's suspicions. As the family trips to help her find personal items increased—a "stolen" sweater turned up tucked away in the back of her closet, and the "disappearing" phone had to be pulled out from behind the bed—we realized most of these "losses" were in Mom's imagination or of her own doing. Maybe there was a thief in the place but most likely not. The truth was we were beginning to think it might be good if someone *did* help themselves from Mom's jam-packed closet and drawers.

It's not as if any of us took stealing lightly or that we were not sympathetic to Mom's feelings. There was simply little we could do. We had made certain nothing of any great value or consequence was left in her room. There was no way to know if what Mom was thinking was valid. Paranoia is hard to watch. Her feelings were real, and we wanted to validate them.

Humor was one way I dealt with my feelings about Mom's growing paranoia. It became a joke around my house. Whenever I couldn't find something, I loudly proclaimed "Miss Sticky Fingers" guilty of larceny in the first degree.

The culprit followed Mom to live at Shirley's house. Shirley confirmed that Mom's habit of hiding things from Miss Sticky Fingers continued, so she had to learn a new version of hide and seek. Mom would hide and Shirley would seek. She found Mom's dentures, hidden in her shoes or flower vases, usually rolled up in napkins. Her purse might be wrapped in a giant towel and hidden in a wastebasket. Under her mattress was a complete storage of jewelry, clothing, books, pictures, and pencils. At night Shirley could hear Mom hiding things and then looking for what she had just hidden.

One evening Mom had suspicions that people were taking food from Shirley's refrigerator not realizing they were sharing the space with her granddaughter who lived in the basement apartment. Shirley thought she had explained it clearly to Mom. A number of days later a bad odor was coming from Mom's room, most noticeably from her closet. It took an extensive search, but there among a stack of bed pads was a package of spoiled steaks. Mom pleaded innocent. *Could Miss Sticky Fingers have resorted to stealing and hiding food?*

Then Mom moved to Avamere in Sherwood, where there were many residents in different stages of Alzheimer's. There was a suspicious character but they didn't call her Miss Sticky Fingers. Her alias was "The Shopper." Remarkably, no one seemed to get upset by her. They just watched her pick up her purse with that "shop 'til I drop" look on her face and said, "Uh oh, it looks like our shopper is on the move again. We'd better keep an eye on her." To her the closets in the various rooms were like different stores. She picked up what she thought she needed and headed for her room, happy with a successful day. With any luck, the folks living in those rooms had marked their clothing. If not, it would be up to the caregivers to sort things out, having made note of the rooms the shopper had visited.

Soon Mom didn't seem to get riled up about those things anymore. Maybe she was looking at it differently. When I looked at some of the unfamiliar things in Mom's closet and desk drawers—like another resident's driver's license—I thought she might have taken on some of that Miss Sticky Fingers identity herself.

25 Dead or Alive

I had been visiting my mother and was heading for the door of the Alzheimer's care facility. As I passed by their chairs, Helen and Myrtle, two other residents, were having quite the discussion about the new dog that was flopped in front of the big television set.

"Well that's the laziest damn dog I've ever seen," Helen said. "I haven't seen it move for over an hour."

"I really think it's dead," Myrtle replied. "What a shame," she added. "It's a very pretty dog."

Helen responded in an irritated voice, "Well, I think a dog should earn its keep like herding sheep or kids or something. Not just lay there."

I was not the only person hearing the conversation. Susan, the morning shift caregiver, stepped up behind the two ladies and rested a hand on each one's shoulder. "Now ladies," she said, "I've told both of you before that the dog is not dead. It is a stuffed animal, a toy dog."

"Of course we know that," Helen said sarcastically.

"Well I just wanted to make sure," Susan said as she walked away.

Both women sat quietly for a few moments. Finally, Myrtle said in a voice a bit quieter than before, "I'm sure I've seen that dog move."

"Well of course you have," Helen snapped. "She just got through saying it wasn't dead."

26 Afternoon Outing

It had been a few days, and I needed to stop in and see Mom, but with Alzheimer's, so often the conversation is the same. She would ask what I'd been doing all day and what "the boss" had been up to. That really meant she couldn't remember my husband Jim's name at that moment.

I would tell her that Jim was working at the School District and her predictable response would be, "I'll bet he's happy keeping busy. He always does such a good job. When you want something done right, you just ask Jim to do it."

I often took Mom for a ride. It didn't seem to matter where we went. She would say, "I just need to get out for a while. It's been eight days since I've been anywhere." I'm not sure where the eight days came from, but it never varied.

Our conversations had become limited in subject. She loved to see animals, and she usually commented on flowers. Some days she could remember the names of the flowers, other days she would just say something about the color. She lost the concept of the seasons, I think. She only knew if it were cold or warm. Other usual comments were about the traffic and the many different kinds of cars in it. She liked white cars. One day she saw an ad somewhere and asked, "What's this '.com' I see? What kind of a word is '.com'? I'm sure my answer just confused her more.

On some days conversation was more difficult than others. Mom asked the same questions repeatedly and seemed to be in a fog. On those days I often put in one of her favorite compact discs. She loved music and liked to sing. Old country music and old hymns were what she liked best. She loved to hear Elvis Presley sing hymns like "The Old Rugged Cross" and "How Great Thou Art." It made me smile because even when I was a kid and many of my friends' parents were condemning Elvis, my Mom liked him. She would say, "Boy can that young man sing, and look at him dance!" She often had a more youthful way of looking at life than the other parents I knew. Somehow, I found great comfort in just being able to sing along with my Mom and Elvis, and in knowing she was content with the afternoon drive.

Other days we would be more adventurous. One day when Mom was living with Shirley in Salem, I took her out for lunch to Mt. Angel, thinking we might find some German sausage and sauerkraut. I didn't really know how to get there so was just heading in the general direction hoping to see the signs I needed. Sensing my uncertainty, Mom asked, "Are we lost?"

"We might be."

"I like getting lost," she responded, "'cause then you don't know where you'll end up. It's always a surprise."

I've heard it said that a contented person is one who enjoys the scenery even while they're on a detour. That would be my mom.

The most memorable part of the trip came totally by accident. As I passed by a farm, I caught sight of a large pig. I slammed on the brakes, backed up, and headed into a driveway by a huge red barn. In front of us was the largest sow I had ever seen. She must have been six feet long. Following close behind her were a dozen little piglets. They trotted along in a straight line behind their mother. Mom just giggled when she saw them.

"Oh look at the curly little tails on those babies. Aren't they so cute? I wish we could see them again," she said as they trotted out of sight.

The pigs were the highlight of the day. We had a good lunch and a nice drive home, but nothing could match the pigs. Mom talked about that trip for several days. Some stories left her quickly, but for some reason this one stayed with her for many tellings. Simple outings can turn into something special. That day we had certainly found the right adventure.

27 Ice-Cream Social

Mom had a nagging cough, so the health nurse at the care facility suggested I take her to the doctor for a routine checkup. Little did we know I would come to pick her up for the appointment at the same time the activity director was there to take the group out for ice cream.

Mom walked out the door with me and was fine until I directed her toward the car instead of the bus. "Why aren't we going with them?" she asked.

"We can't do that today," I answered. "You have a doctor's appointment so we won't be able to go for ice cream."

She hesitated a bit but then got into the car.

"Well I want to go for ice cream," she said adamantly.

"Mom, we've made an appointment with the doctor," I said in my most matter-of-fact voice.

"Who decided I needed a doctor? I should decide that, not someone else."

"Yes I know, Mom, but they thought the doctor should check out that cough." It was time to use that "they" word. I used it often to take the blame off me and put it on the authoritative group I called "they."

We were on the road now, but Mom was not happy about it. "You get to go to the doctor today," I said again, hoping to get her usual positive response about doctor visits. "You've always liked this doctor." But she was not going to be distracted this time.

"I want to go have ice cream with my friends. I have the right to have ice cream if I want it."

My patience was wearing thin. I was in no mood for two-year-old stubbornness or even an adolescent need to be with her friends. "I'm sorry, but we are going to the doctor. You can have ice cream another day."

"I want to go with my friends to have ice cream today!"

"You know what, Mom, that is enough about ice cream. I don't want to hear another word about it." I felt like I was talking to one of my children, certainly not my mother. "We can go for ice cream when we finish with the doctor," I added. She finally stopped complaining but sat with arms crossed and a pout on her face. She didn't say anything until I parked the car at the clinic.

"*They* should not decide if I want to go with my friends or go to the doctor," she said, almost to herself. "*I* should decide."

My heart softened as I got her walker out of the back seat. *I shouldn't get angry with her. She just wants to be in control of her own life. So what if she's acting like a spoiled child? She has a right to be frustrated.*

The incident faded as she told the doctor how good she was feeling. He looked at me and I nodded my head yes at the same time she said, "No, I don't think I have a bad cough." He listened to her lungs and she began coughing even as he examined her.

We picked up a prescription and headed for the car.

As we drove away from the clinic I asked, "Do you want to stop now and get some ice cream?"

"Maybe a piece of lemon pie," she said. "I don't really feel like ice cream today."

Hmmm.

From Mom's Journal:

Patience is a virtue.

28 Four-legged Friends

As with much of the elderly population, pets can be a welcome sight to a person with Alzheimer's disease. There is no doubt how important the little dog QC was in Mom's life when she lived with my sister. What counts is the unconditional love pets can give. They are not complicated and confusing to those dealing with Alzheimer's disease. I believe many animals have a sense for a person's condition. My kitten usually wanted to bite and play, but when put on Mom's lap she relaxed and took a nap while Mom stroked her fur.

When I was searching for a facility for Mom, I noted that more than one of the Alzheimer's units had resident dogs or cats. Individuals owned some animals and others belonged to the facility. I met a golden retriever named Meg who I was told had come to the rescue many times. She was a loyal member of the staff who could be called on day or night to lie beside an upset or irritated human resident and calm a bad situation.

If there is a socialized animal in your family, it could be a huge treat for the Alzheimer's patients to have a visit. Of course, as in all things, it may not be a treat to all residents. If a person traditionally disliked animals or was not accepting of pets earlier in their lives, that is unlikely to change. But for those who do enjoy animals, it can be a fun activity to bring your dog and a bucket of soap and water to give your dog a bath on a warm sunny day. With chairs arranged in a circle on the lawn or courtyard, residents will be entertained watching the process. It will provide a simple distraction in an otherwise uneventful day. It is important to make sure the facility welcomes animals and gives permission to bring your animal guest.

Another thing to remember is that the animal does not have to be real. Remember how that old teddy bear was such a comfort to you when you were a child? Because we don't know where your loved one might be in his or her mind at any given time, that teddy bear, monkey, or stuffed tiger might be just the moral support he or she needs to get through a long, frightening night. While Mom was at Avamere, they had a large soft stuffed dog that laid in front of the television most of the time. The residents loved it. Occasionally I saw a caregiver put it on the couch by a lonely resident or just give it a hug himself. Everyone needs a friend to hug from time to time.

Keep in mind that this is not the place for expensive dolls, bears, or treasured collections. Most facilities have an open-door policy, and wandering residents are known to pick up things they find attractive—whether it's theirs or not. Caregivers have busy days. Keeping track of such personal items should not be expected. Only take items you are willing to lose. That mindset will help you deal with upsetting disappearances.

29 Ah, Spring!

It was a gorgeous spring afternoon and I thought I would stop in at Avamere to see how Mom was doing. When I didn't see her sitting in her usual spot on the love seat, I asked the caregiver where she was "hiding." The caregiver chuckled because hiding things is common in the Alzheimer's unit: dolls, purses, silverware, other people's glasses... "Oh, she and Sam are in the back dining room," she responded. I liked that back dining room because it was light and open. I'm sure that is what often prompted Mom to sit there. Another attraction was the busy street outside the window. Lately there had been much to watch as construction crews had finished the GI Joe store across the way, and other smaller shops were now being completed. So much action!

So there she sat with Sam, chairs close together, taking in all the happenings outside. I pulled up my own chair and sat beside Mom. They were both pleased to see me, although they had looked quite content when I walked up. "What's going on?" I asked.

"Oh we're just watching the day go by," she said, a phrase she had used for as long as I could remember. "It looks like a new store over there. It can't be very far to walk. We should walk over there one of these days."

The ever-agreeable Sam answered, "Well yes we should. We should walk over there one of these days."

It isn't very far, I thought, *but it would wear the two of you out.*
We sat as if on benches in the park and watched a young
woman pushing a baby stroller. The little boy in the stroller was
obviously enjoying the ride in the warm spring air. His sister
hopped and skipped alongside, talking and giggling as she went.
"Oh look at that cute little baby," Mom said. "I wish she would
bring it right over here so we could hold it."

"Wouldn't that be nice," agreed Sam. "She could bring it right
over so we could hold it."

Out on the street a truck pulling a camper trailer rolled by.
"Wow, that was a nice trailer. We used to have fun camping,
didn't we Mom?" I asked, hoping to get a reaction from her.

"Yes, we did, but I don't think it was that fancy kind of
camping."

I asked Sam, "Do you like to go camping?"

"Oh yes," he responded quickly. "I like to camp by the water."
Obviously it was something he had done somewhere in his
past.

"I like to be by the water too," I said, and we smiled at each
other, recognizing something in common.

Mom commented, "Well, Sam, that's something we haven't
done in all the years we've been together. We should do that
maybe next week. We'll go camping."

Mr. Agreeable said, "Yes, we should do that next week. We
should go camping."

Not one to rain on anyone's parade, I agreed. "It sounds like
fun to me."

We talked a little more about this and that. I left the two as I
had found them, thoroughly enjoying their simple afternoon.

The reality of it all is that Mom and Sam had not been
together for years. Indeed, not together at all. They would not
be walking to the new store or camping together. But you know,
it was a beautiful spring day, and it was fun to sit there on the

make-believe park bench with those two daydreamers and plan summer outings, no matter how unrealistic. As the popular GI Joe's ad said, "Seize the moment."

Is it real or pretend?

Does it matter in the end?

Accept the joy in each moment.

30 Dorothy

When Dorothy came to Avamere, they settled her in the same room as Mom. Mom had not had a roommate up to that point. Though we had discussed it with the administration from time to time, it was not until then that we felt she was ready. It looked like a good match. We all watched closely to see how things would go. Though they didn't pay much attention to each other, they seemed to be comfortable and neither bothered the other one's things. A common attitude of *hands off my stuff* was necessary to both women.

Dorothy appeared to be one of those down-to-earth people who had probably worked hard in her life. She was quite agitated when she first came. Like many others, she was unhappy to be taken from her home and forced to live in this strange environment. She was not open to being told when, where, and what to eat or when to go to bed. Her adjustment was difficult. When I came to see Mom, Dorothy often asked me if I could give her a ride somewhere or at least get the door unlocked so she could get out and go home. One day early in her stay she again expressed her desire to leave, saying she had pets to care for and her family needed her. I tried to comfort her by saying that I was sure there were people taking care of things for her and she shouldn't be concerned about it. This was a good place where she could relax and not worry. It was the wrong thing to say to this woman—way too condescending.

She put her face close to mine and in a metered, angry voice said, "That-is-so-much-bullshit!" *Ooookay...* I backed off, a bit speechless. Obviously, I had equated her condition with some of the other residents, and I was way off base. Each person in this facility was different and needed to be responded to as such. I doubt that Dorothy had been the helpless type throughout her lifetime, and she didn't need anyone making her feel that way now. It put me in my place.

From that day on Dorothy and I got along well. Her favorite spot to relax was in the recliner by the door. She would sit with a cup of coffee and loved to visit with anyone who would stop and chat. Almost every time I came through, she asked what I was doing. I'd say that I came to see my mother, and she would ask who that was. "Oh, you're Ruthie's daughter. That's nice." If Mom happened to be sitting near her, Mom would introduce me then as her daughter.

If I said, "Yes, Mom, I know your roommate Dorothy," she would say, "Oh, is she my roommate?" I can't tell you how many times we went through that scenario. I don't know if they ever realized they were roommates.

One day when I mentioned to Dorothy that I was canning tomatoes and peaches, she picked right up on that. "My mother and I used to can," she told me. "We lived in Montana and many times the weather would be too cold to make it into town. It was good to have food on the shelves in the winter. I know canning is hard work." This is the puzzlement of Alzheimer's disease. One minute these roommates were introducing me and themselves to each other, and the next minute Dorothy was remembering clearly the cold weather and the lifestyle of Montana in winter.

I enjoyed the conversations with Dorothy. Anyone passing through quickly without taking the time to stop and talk to her missed the treasures she recounted of her colorful life. That's a shame. She still had wonderful stories to share.

Unfortunately, Dorothy had been a heavy smoker all her life. Her lungs and heart were damaged. She had a setback—congestive heart failure—and had to go to the care home. I missed seeing her. Since Mom hadn't really gotten the fact that she was her roommate, I doubt she noticed when Dorothy was gone.

31 No Way Home

Alzheimer's disease
No way to return home now
Suspended in time

The above is my weak attempt at haiku. I haven't really figured it out yet. Haiku has a pattern but the rules around it seem loose, each verse having its own personality. It may be a strange comparison, but it makes me think of Alzheimer's disease: unpredictable. There is a saying in the Alzheimer's community, "If you have met one person with Alzheimer's you have met one person with Alzheimer's," the point being that the disease affects each person differently. However, in one of the stages of Alzheimer's there is a time when each person will follow a pattern and ask relentlessly, "When can I go home?" The problem with the question is that there is no way of knowing where that person considers *home*. It is seldom the home they just moved out of, the home where they lived with a spouse and raised a family. Most often, they will be talking about a home in their childhood. It is the one where they lived with their mother and father. Perhaps it's really a comfort zone they want to return to.

For a year early in her dementia, my mother lived with my sister in a white, wood-framed house in Salem. During much of that time, I think, in Mom's mind it was the small white house in South Superior, Wisconsin, where she lived with her parents, brothers, and sisters. She was living in her early adolescent years. She often sang little songs in Swedish, the language spoken in her childhood home. None of us knew what she was singing, but her smiling face told us they were happy tunes. She talked of going to the factory where her father worked. With a little twinkle in her eyes she would say words mocking the Swedish lilt, "Yah, I tink I need to go dere now." In her mind, I'm sure she could see herself and her sister skipping along the railroad tracks on their way to meet their father returning from work.

Also in that span of time, she did many art projects with my sister and niece. She drew flowers and happy animal pictures. Even her creativity was at a child's level. Shirley took wonderful care of her and would "go" with Mom to whatever place in time her mind took her on a given day. I truly believe because of this atmosphere of openness and love, she was comfortable being a child again.

It was an interesting time for our family because we saw a part of our mother we hadn't really known before. She had seldom spoken of her childhood, something I now regret having asked little about. We saw a small picture of her past and what "home" meant to her at that time in her life. Though she couldn't return there, it seems to have been a pleasant time of life for her.

One has to look hard for the few blessings to be gained from Alzheimer's disease, but our family can be thankful for this one.

Looking back in time
Memories are ours alone
Which ones do you choose?

32 Rabbits and Raccoons

My friend Jean's mom was in a different care facility than my mom, but the buildings were similar in structure. In a hallway where all the doors can look the same, sometimes it's hard for the elderly resident to tell which one is theirs. In Mom's case, a small picture of her and the little dog QC marked her doorway. To help her mom locate her room, Jean decided on a small cast-iron rabbit to put beside her door. One day when Jean went to visit, the rabbit was not outside the door but resting comfortably inside her mom's room. Jean asked why the rabbit was not in the hallway. Her mom answered without hesitation, "It's too cold outside for any poor animal."

Jean reminded her mother that the animal was not real and the hallway was not really outside. Her mother replied, "So what? It can still get cold!" These are the moments when logic does not prevail and an argument will get no one anywhere but upset. She was right anyway. The rabbit could still get cold.

It reminded me of how my mom used to talk to the two raccoon boot brushes I had at the doorway in my garage. Each time she came to the house she would say, "Oh, you little animals are so cute; I wish I could pet you." She said it with a smile and a little wave of her hand. Who could tell if she knew what they were? It doesn't really matter.

33 Escape to Todos Santos

A page from my journal:

Today as I write here beside the pool listening to the waterfall, a dog lying companionably beside the chair, my mother sits in the living room of a care facility in Oregon. The residents there all suffer with Alzheimer's disease, the great social leveler. Their once active, diverse lives are now disintegrating memories. Few can join in meaningful conversation. Each one lives in a world of his or her own.

When I told Mom I was leaving for a writing workshop in Mexico the following day, she said simply, "That's a good idea." Nothing close to the flood of comments and questions she would have had in her younger years. Mom had a love for travel, and with an hour to pack was ready to go anywhere. She and I had taken great trips together, and in earlier days her first and last questions would have been, "Can I come along?"

Mom would have loved Todos Santos, with its quiet village atmosphere and brightly painted houses. She had an attraction for the tanned skin, coal-black hair, and shining brown eyes of the Mexican people. Before Alzheimer's disease, my mother would have been flirting unabashedly with every male shopkeeper and waiter she encountered.

Not interested in spending even one half-hour at writing, her day would have been spent exploring, walking to the beach, and at least two trips into town. The rutted roads and massive mud puddles would not have deterred her treks in this new and charming environment.

I guess I may as well admit it. Mother has come here with me. Because I am so connected to her life and her condition, I cannot escape her. I must write my way through it. I surrender to that.

So indeed, have I gotten away from anything, or have I traveled to Todos Santos to become even more intimately connected than ever before? Thoughts do come with clarity here.

The only remedy I see is to put more words together that might help and encourage others and myself through this predicament in life, called Alzheimer's disease.

34 Cassie

The tiny kitten curled contentedly on Mom's lap. Cassie had come to me, orphaned, at four weeks old. I bottle-fed and cuddled her. Her full name came to me as she showed her independent nature. She would be called Sassy Cassie. At this moment, however, she didn't look sassy at all. She resembled a limp rag doll. It was that total relaxation thing cats can do and humans can only envy.

Mom was at my house to have lunch and to spend some time visiting with my sister and me. As we prepared the food, I put the kitten in Mom's lap to keep her occupied for a few minutes. Since Cassie loved attention and most folks with Alzheimer's seem to love animals, it was a good fit. Conversation was getting harder for Mom, but it didn't stop her from asking (at least ten times) where I got the kitten and was there another one she could have. My answer was that the cat was given to me and I would see if there was one more at Peg's house for her. With the sincere honesty of a child, Mom assured me over and over again that she could take good care of it.

As Mom rubbed her little striped face, Cassie responded with a contented squirm that said, *More, more.* Mom caressed the kitten, seeming to measure each pointed ear, going over them several times. Her fingers let the kitten's legs slide through and then stopped to count each toe, each claw. Cassie purred

Cassie, the quintessential cat, relaxing on Ruth's lap. We know kittens love attention and folks with Alzheimer's usually like the company of a small animal.

happily. I could imagine her thinking this woman was surely sent to give her all the adoration every cat deserves.

Mom's wrinkled hands had covered almost every inch of the kitten's body. Cassie's tail was the last to get the inspection. As Mom checked the sleeping cat's small limp tail and let it fall back to her lap she proclaimed her approval. "This cat has everything she needs."

35 Candy and Cement. They Both Start with C...

Mom sat on the bench in the courtyard with fellow resident Sam. They were enjoying one of the few warm days we had had this spring. Susan (a caregiver), Kelly (the maintenance man), and I were looking over the formal landscaping. "You know, this is a great area," Susan said, "but we need some color out here, something to make it more cheerful." We discussed flower boxes that the residents could use for a garden. We thought hanging baskets would be nice. Kelly said he could put in posts for those.

I jumped in and said, "I've been making some steppingstones that are kind of fun. I'd be glad to bring down a couple."

"Better yet, Susan said, "could the residents make the stones as an activity?"

"Sure," I agreed, feeling ever so helpful. "I'll bring down all the supplies, and we'll do six small ones."

We asked Mom and Sam if they thought that was a good idea. Both agreed, as they "liked being busy." In reality, they probably didn't have a clue what we were talking about.

Thursday came and I arrived at Avamere with buckets and pre-measured cement. I had set up little kits for each stone and brought along some extra goodies so that the residents could be as creative as they felt comfortable being. There were bright colored plastic geometric shapes, pink plastic butterflies, smooth black river rock, and a few pieces of bright-colored glass. I had smoothed out the edges on the glass so there would be no chance of cutting oneself. I felt I had done a reasonably good job of preparation.

The caregivers picked six residents who seemed interested and set them down at the table in the dining area where we had covered everything with a thick layer of newspaper. I was going to mix the cement in the small bucket and pour it into the molds. Then people could use the pieces I had set out for them, or they could create their own pattern. I laid the spare pieces in the center of the table.

Before I could get the cement in the first mold, my mother was trying to eat one of the black rocks. "No, Mom, that's a rock." I said a bit frantically.

"It looks like licorice," she answered.

"It's a rock." I countered.

"Well, I'd rather have licorice," she said, a bit irritated. "Why would anyone put rocks on the table where we eat?"

Not a bad question for someone with Alzheimer's, I thought. *She might be thinking more clearly than I am.*

I explained again what we were doing. She seemed to accept it but not happily, probably still thinking about her favorite licorice. About that time one of the men—another candy lover, I presume—started to put a piece of red glass into his mouth. The caregiver stopped him just in time.

I was a little shaken, taken off guard by this behavior. *What in the world was I thinking? This could have been dangerous. I should have known better! Well we've got the goofy cement mixed now. We may as well keep going.*

Two caregivers helped, and we finally got the project started in the right direction. Not one person used the kits I had set up for them. They were having their own fun. A couple of people took the caregivers' suggestion and put their handprints in the stones. In another surprise move, one resident decided to lick

"Original design" stepping stones similar to those made by the residents of Avamere.

the cement off her fingers. Thanks goodness for alert, fast-moving caregivers. We finished with no further incidents.

"Boy, this was a fun craft idea, wasn't it?" I remarked, a bit discouraged.

"Oh, it's just another day at Avamere," Susan said cheerfully. "And it's great to have something different for the folks to do."

I went home questioning the whole idea.

A couple of days later it was time to take the stones out of the molds and clean them up. They did turn out colorful and fun after all. Some of the residents came along to the courtyard to help us decide where to put the steppingstones. Not one remembered having made them. Since they had put their names on them, they agreed they probably had done the job, and they were pleased. We all thought they looked nice. The caregiver said, "Well, that was fun and the stones are a cheerful addition. Want to do six more in a couple of weeks?"

Hesitating at first but feeling better now about my little craft project, I said, "Sure. Why not?" Working with this group had been a challenge, but rewarding. Okay, it was even kind of fun.

I gathered my materials and said good-bye to Mom. As I walked away I thought I heard her say, "They look good enough to eat."

From Mom's Journal:

> *Develop some humility. Be willing to listen and learn from everyone you meet.*

36 Fine Dining

Here I sit at McDonald's. It's been a long time since I frequented this place. My kids are all grown up and moved away. I thought except for the occasional trip when my grandchildren visit or I'm hit by a craving for French fries I was not going to be seen sitting inside again. But here I am and what a treat it is for me today.

Mom still loves her hamburgers.

I think we all have to indulge in a good old juicy burger once in a while. It's part of that kid who remains in each of us. Well with Alzheimer's, Mom had that "kid thing" for sure—some days more than others. Often I picked up a burger at lunchtime and took it to Avamere for Mom. Add a strawberry milkshake and she was definitely eating gourmet! On the day I wrote the above journal entry, the idea had struck to take her to McDonald's with me.

Little did I guess what fun this would be for her. We took the wheelchair right into the play area full of kids. Since my grandchildren live so far away, I seldom have small children to take for visits to Mom. Let me tell you, I hit the jackpot. Kids were running and screaming and climbing, coming back to their table for a few bites, then more running and screaming and climbing. Did I say I was enjoying this? Yes, but it wasn't the kids' fun I was enjoying but my mom's. She was taking it all in.

"Oh look at that cute little one! He's so high up there! Do you see him?" "Maybe she shouldn't push so hard on that net; she might fall!" All the while, her eyes were shining and her smile was wide. I had to remind her to eat.

The only downside was that many kids don't really see old folks like Mom often. They were afraid or uneasy when she reached out to touch them. Some of the moms understood and encouraged their child to say hello. Some moms were uncomfortable themselves. That's understandable. It's not the same world I grew up in where grandparents and older aunts, uncles, and friends lived nearby and visited often. But with so much busyness and commotion around, their reserve was hardly noticeable to Mom. She was having a good time just watching them.

Like the kids from their play, Mom got tired from the noise and stimulation. By the time she finished her lunch I could see she had had enough. (Me too.) When I took Mom back to Avamere she couldn't wait to tell the other residents about all the kids and the action. One would think we had gone on a great adventure. She got to see some kids and have her special lunch, and I enjoyed seeing many smiles.

Who knew this would be such a great outing? We'll do this again.

37 Distorted Time/Distorted Truths

*M*y mother's fragile fingers follow the outline of the white flower pattern on the dress draping over her knees. The freshly painted fingernails testify to the visit of the young volunteers from the Middle School. It must have been "beauty day" yesterday. Mom usually picks bright red when asked what color she prefers for her nails, and sure enough that's what I see today.

"I'm wearing Elvira's dress," she said as she brushed lunch crumbs from her lap.

"Oh you are," I said. "Well it looks nice on you."

It was a lovely blue against her pale skin—a good color for her. I had thought so when I picked it out at Value Village a few weeks earlier. Current fashion made it hard to find simple wash and wear dresses for Mom so more often than not I got what I needed at secondhand stores. She refused to wear pants. Mom was obsessed with this particular dress at the time, wanted to wear it every day, keeping the caregivers busy getting it into the laundry each night.

"How is Elvira?" Mom asked.

"I haven't seen her for a while," I answered, "But she was fine when I did."

This was a true statement, however the last time I had seen my aunt was about forty years earlier. She died five years after that. No use to elaborate all that to Mom. On this day she was living in that world of forty years ago when a sister might bring over a dress she no longer wore. No harm done. On another day Mom might say, "Elvira is gone, isn't she?" Then I would answer, "Yes, Mom; Auntie's been gone a long time." I'd quickly change the subject unless she seemed to need to talk about it, which was seldom the case.

Each day can be a different time frame with many who suffer from Alzheimer's disease. We have to stay open to change our thinking to match theirs.

A caregiver related another such story to me. It was about a woman, now confined to a wheelchair, whose granddaughter often visited her. For some reason, each visit would leave the woman crying and depressed. It was puzzling until the caregiver overheard part of the conversation between the two.

"Who is feeding my horses?" the woman asked her granddaughter.

"Grandma, you know you don't have horses anymore. You can't take care of them. You need to stop asking that question. The horses are gone." The woman's face fell, and she looked down at her hands, confused and near tears.

During the next visit, the caregiver suggested to the granddaughter that she not say such things about the horses as it was depressing her grandmother. The visitor's stern answer was clear. She would not "lie" to her grandmother. She felt her grandmother needed to know and accept the truth, not hear lies. The visits continued with the same sad results.

The caregiver decided to intervene in her own way.

After the granddaughter left, she struck up a conversation with the grandmother, mentioning that she had heard the family purchased some beautiful grass hay from eastern Oregon. "The horses are eating well."

Now she was talking the woman's language and calming her concerns. She did not say *your* horses; she said *the* horses—if you want to get technical. It was enough to reassure the woman that *horses* were being fed.

When are lies truly lies? We all know the difference. With compassion, we must remember that in the world in which this person resides, truth is where their minds are on a particular day. We have to go to the space in time where they exist to be able to tell the truth.

I doubt a caring God will judge you for what at times may feel like a fabrication. My thought is you will be blessed for joining in that time distortion and giving an Alzheimer's sufferer a sense of well-being.

From Mom's Journal:

> *People will forget what you said*
> *People will forget what you did.*
> *But they will never forget*
> *How you made them feel.*

38 Simple Wisdom

While visiting the doctor for a checkup, Mom asked the nurse if the doctor was a nice person. The nurse answered, "Yes, she is very nice person. If she wasn't, I wouldn't work for her."

Mom got a funny look on her face. After the nurse left, Mom repeated the comment. "If she wasn't I wouldn't work for her."

I was curious about what she was thinking, so I asked her if she had ever worked for someone who wasn't nice. She said, "Oh yes, that's for sure, but there were times when I didn't have the option to work for only nice people."

I could only agree with that.

"But those mean bosses didn't get our best did they?" Mom said, more a statement than a question. I liked her logic. I'm sure Mom worked hard at any job she had. What she was saying clearly, even with Alzheimer's disease, was that those mean bosses didn't get the best of her spirit.

39 Nationality Still Counts

My mother, Ruth Matilda Samuelson, definitely was a Swede. Every once in a while she would start talking with a Swedish accent. "Yah, I tink it's time to do dat," would come rolling off her tongue. Even though the Swedish language is all but lost in our family, we still carry a pride in our heritage. It was a part of Mom's identity that Alzheimer's could not steal.

One day when we were talking about traveling, I said I would like to go to Sweden. She informed me that she didn't have to go to Sweden. She was already a Swede.

Another day, she asked where her dog had gone. She didn't have a dog and hadn't for a long time, but I just answered that he must have gone visiting. She asked if we had a dog, and I said no, that we had been looking for one. When she asked what kind, I said Norwegian elkhound. Still feeling that age-old competition between the Norwegians and the Swedes, she quickly asked "Norwegian elkhound? Why not Swedish elkhound?"

40 Sticky Situations

If you thought dealing with teenagers and their romantic crushes and relationships was fun, you are going to get a real kick out of romance Alzheimer's style. As in all affairs of the heart there can be jealousy, love triangles, and a significant amount of frustration. The situation can get touchy and complicated for the caregivers when there is a spouse involved.

Because the residents spend so much time together and many are lonely or afraid, it is quite normal that they might be drawn to someone they see everyday for comfort and companionship. We saw it first early in Mom's stay at Avamere. The attraction was between a man (formerly a practicing physician) and a woman who arrived shortly after he moved into the facility.

I never saw the woman's husband but heard her refusing his phone calls. She often wanted to leave the facility but never asked to go home with him. Hard to tell what the history was there, real or imagined.

The former doctor had a nice, attractive wife. She came to the facility often and took her husband out for ice cream and walks. Yet for some reason when the female resident was in the room, his eyes often searched for her, and sometimes he would start to get up to greet her. His wife would stop him, and you could see she was upset. She tried to be understanding, but it was obvious that it saddened her heart. She knew there was nothing to do about it. To spare her feelings, the caregivers kept the doctor and his lady friend apart as much as possible, especially when they knew his wife was coming in.

My mom enjoyed the company of a man. I think she felt safer in that space. A special friendship developed between her and Sam. They smiled and talked to each other all the time. Soon they were sitting next to one another holding hands. Then it got so they wanted to give each other little kisses when one or the other would leave the facility. It became a real problem for Sam's family, especially his wife. She would be angry every time she came to visit and saw them together. She insisted the caregivers keep them apart. They tried to carry out her wishes. This agitated my mother who had been a jealous and possessive woman when it came to *her* men. Mom thought the wife was coming to steal her friend. In her head she had Sam mixed up with her friend Jerry from the assisted living home where she had lived before Avamere. In fact, she would often call Sam "Jerry."

From my side of the story, Sam was company for Mom and gave her someone to talk to and a reason to feel good about herself. Sam enjoyed her company and he seemed contented when he was with her. Though I was selfishly okay with the situation, Sam's wife was furious. She came to one support group meeting, saw me, and didn't come again. I had hoped she and I could talk it over, but she refused to talk to me. As if I could do anything about it! My mother had Alzheimer's disease, but she was just as stubborn as she had ever been. There was much discussion with the caregivers and the administrator by me and by Sam's wife. It turned out to be more disruptive to try to keep them separated than to let them quietly enjoy each other's company. I knew one day it would come to a scene.

I had taken Mom to my home for an afternoon. We had a pleasant early dinner. It was dusk and time for Mom to return to the facility. We were already on the sidewalk heading in when I saw them coming out of the building. Too late to run! We were going to have to come face to face with Sam, his wife, and their grown son. I started talking to Mom about anything I could think of, hoping to distract her, but to no avail.

"Oh, there's my sweetie," she said.

"Hi, Ruthie," Sam said, waving his hand enthusiastically like a child. "Where have you been so long?" He held his hand out to greet her.

"Did you miss me?" she asked as she gave him a little kiss on the cheek. Oh dear. If looks from his wife were a dagger, our hearts would have been bleeding on the sidewalk.

"Come on, Mom. We need to get inside," I said, but she wasn't moving. No one was moving.

Sam said to me, "Have you met my wife and my son?" I couldn't truly appreciate his politeness at this juncture. Mom appeared not to have heard a word he said. She patted his cheek and completely ignored everyone else.

"Where are you going now?" she asked oh-so-sweetly.

Thoroughly uncomfortable, I held out my hand and said, "It's nice to meet you both." There was no response to my hand or my greeting. I wanted to melt into the cement under my feet, but there would be no melting in the frigid atmosphere surrounding this moment.

Sam's wife answered Mom's question angrily, "We're going to dinner." She grabbed his arm and directed him toward the car. Their son walked behind them.

As our eyes met I said, "I'm sorry about all this," but his look was not one of understanding. He was openly disgusted.

At least Mom was moving again. "See you when you get back," she called with a little wave.

"Okay I'll see you later," Sam responded lightly.

Neither of them was affected whatsoever by the situation. How could anyone take it seriously? This was just an innocent, childlike relationship. These two were in no way wanting to hurt anyone. They lived in a different world. I was sure my Mom didn't realize the consequences of who that woman was. Then just as I had myself almost convinced, Mom said in a slightly mocking tone of voice, "I'll bet our dinner was a lot better than theirs is going to be."

Was she talking about food? I doubt it.

From a greeting card:

> *Sometimes the best thing to do (in fact the only thing to do) is just sit down and laugh.*
> —Mary Anne Radmacher-Hersey

41 Memory that Comes and Goes

Mom threw me another curve. I was happy about it, but it reminded me once again that I could not predict how she was going to handle any circumstance. She recognized my son visiting from California. *No big deal,* you might say, but in this case it was a surprise.

A few weeks earlier, our daughter Tami and her two sons had been here from Japan. It wasn't a long visit, but we made sure to visit Mom at the Alzheimer's facility where she was living. Mom hadn't seen Tami's youngest boy, Ari, so we were excited for her to meet him, as well as seeing Tami and her older boy, Sevien, for the first time in a couple of years.

There were the usual polite greetings and hugs, but it was obvious Mom didn't realize who she was talking to. I tried to help her connect with Tami by telling her about Tami's long trip to come here and that this was her new little boy. Mom struggled with trying to remember. It seemed to irritate her that she didn't know what or who I was talking about. It was painful for Tami, as Mom had admired her adventures and was ever ready to hear of the new places Tami traveled. Nothing worked. Mom even got a little cranky with the boys, asking whose kids were playing with her walker. Not the usual loving grandmother Tami knew. We kept our visit short since it hadn't proved to be a positive one. Tami didn't say much as we drove home. I felt hard-pressed to explain. It was not what I had expected.

Two days later when I visited Mom again and told her Tami was on her way back to Japan she asked, "How come I didn't get to see her?" I told her Tami had come down to see her. She looked so sad. "Gee, I'm sorry I missed her," was all she could say. Then she asked, "How far is Japan? Will she have a long drive? I hope I get to see her next time she comes." I remember thinking, *I hope so too, Mom.*

About five weeks later our oldest boy, Greg, came to visit. He wanted to see Mom, but had many other plans as well. One day I told him I would bring Mom up to our house to make it easier for him. Whenever it fit in his schedule that afternoon, she would be there. My sister Marge was visiting from Montana, and we would just chat with Mom until Greg got there. I reminded him at least twice that his grandmother might not recognize him. I wish I had warned Tami. I didn't want Greg to feel the same disappointment she had.

That day Mom seemed to be thinking quite clearly as we waited for Greg to arrive from his friend's home. When he walked in, Mom said, with no coaching, "Well there's my Gregor boy," the same way she had greeted him most of his life. All my warnings had been unnecessary. Marge and I looked at each other in shock. Greg knelt in front of his grandmother and began telling her about his family and about his recent trip to Greece. She listened intently and even asked questions while Marge and I stood by, nearly in tears. I'm sure Greg thought I had been exaggerating Mom's condition.

Later I tried to determine what made the difference between the two visits. Most importantly, I think it was better to have had Mom in our house where she expected to see certain people. Tami and her boys had been out of context at Avamere. Tami may have been more recognizable to Mom in our home. Secondly, Greg is six years older than Tami. In Mom's mind, Tami was not a grown woman with children of her own. She

**Bonnie's son Greg having an eye level
visit with his grandmother.**

was still Grandma's little girl. Mom seemed to look at Deanna, Shirley's youngest daughter, in much the same way. Greg was the oldest and most serious of our three children and had seemed more mature than others his age. Mom expected him to be an adult with children.

The opposite reaction to the two grandchildren just threw me. Two years earlier, her comments to our six-foot-two middle son, Tim, had been predictable. She teased, "Look how tall you are now, but I remember holding and rocking you when you were just a tiny boy." That had been much earlier in her Alzheimer's journey. At that time, there was memory left that she could count on. Now each day was different. Nothing was predictable, and the rest of us just had to learn to live with it and wonder.

42 E is for Eye Doctor

"Look into my eyes," he said with a warm, caring voice.
"I could look at those beautiful brown eyes anytime," she responded coyly.

Sound like the beginning of a romantic interlude? Well, no, it was my unabashedly flirtatious eighty-five-year-old mother Ruth having her eyes examined. This was our first visit with this doctor, and he was completely taken off guard. Ruth had been diagnosed with Alzheimer's disease two years earlier. Though the disease had taken its toll on her, it had not suppressed her friendly personality. It reminded me of an email a friend sent to my sister: "I got to laughing when I got off the phone thinking about your sweet mom. I sure hope God's wife isn't the jealous type. When your mom enters the gate to heaven, I just know she is going to flirt with Him." As a younger person I would have shuddered at the kind of remarks Mom made, but by that time I simply smiled as the somewhat flustered doctor collected his thoughts.

The doctor asked me about her history and what had caused me to bring her in.

I reported that she had been showing signs of poor eyesight. She held cards and photos at odd angles moving them as if she might see them better in a different light. She seemed unable to read the newspapers and magazines she customarily enjoyed. I wasn't sure if it was bad eyesight or the Alzheimer's disease making the difference. At first she had denied the problem but later admitted she was having trouble seeing.

"She has thick cataracts in both eyes," the doctor remarked after examining her. "They should have been removed before now. It would have been better if you had not waited. How long has it been since her eyes were examined?"

I felt my face flush. Anger, frustration, and guilt all washed over me at once. *How long had it been? We've had so many other problems the last two years. How could I have overlooked her eyes?*

"She has had pneumonia and a hip fracture." I spoke as I tried to recall. "Yes, it was before her Alzheimer's diagnosis. At that time, she saw an eye doctor at Kaiser. They said she did have cataracts but that they were not *ripe* enough yet. I remember that word because I thought it an odd way to describe an eye problem." I was still trying to justify myself to him. "Her condition makes it hard to tell what is going on in her head. She denied having any problems at all until I kept questioning her. It's only been in the last month that I noticed her struggling."

I knew I sounded offended, and that's how I felt. I'd been trying to do everything right with Mom. I had not ignored any of her needs intentionally.

"Certain steroid medications encourage cataract growth," he said in a less accusatory tone. "Let's evaluate what she can see."

He put his hand on her shoulder and said, "Ruth, let's focus on the big *E*."

"What's the *E* got that I haven't got?" she teased. This time the doctor was not so surprised at her remark.

"Nothing at all, Ruth; I just want to know if you can see it," he answered with a slight smile.

"Oh sure; I can see the *E*. Not much else, maybe a couple of other letters."

Then he asked a question that took me by surprise. "Will it make a valid difference in Ruth's life to improve her eyesight?"

I answered adamantly, "Yes! She has always loved to read. I want her to be able to pick up a magazine or newspaper and be able to see it. She needs to see pictures of far-off grandchildren. It may not mean a great deal to her for much longer, but let's give her the ability to see as long as she can. Her world gets smaller every day as it is."

The doctor understood. We scheduled surgery.

Surgery day was confusing for Mom. I had recruited my sisters for moral support for her and for me. Not really understanding what was going on, Mom still sensed our apprehension. As we waited she started reciting the twenty-third Psalm, which was a little unnerving for us girls. The tension was broken when she recited, "Thy rod and thy reel, they comfort me."

When we laughed and corrected her, she covered herself well by saying, "Well, you know fishing can be a comforting thing." She amazed me with her quick answers at the oddest times. Her sense of humor and wit were sometimes spared from the ravages of Alzheimer's.

The surgery did not go well. With cataract surgery the patient is only partially sedated, needing to be awake and alert enough to follow instructions given by the doctor and anesthesiologist. Being quiet and still are most important. That is something that was near impossible for my mother even before Alzheimer's days.

The cataract was thick and tough. Because of the difficult situation, there was a tear that would require another procedure.

Mom was unable to see much of anything for the next few days as we waited for the tear to heal. She was understandably paranoid and cranky. She wanted to know what in the world I was doing to her. My reassurance that it was going to get better was no comfort to her. Her normal lack of confidence in my medical savvy was transparent. My own confidence was shaken as well. I had not expected any problems. Now not only could she not read, she couldn't see the chair to sit down. She could barely see her food to eat. We had come to a real low spot with nothing to do to change a bad situation but wait for brighter days—in more ways than one.

43 Music for the Eyes

The lyrics of "The Old Rugged Cross" rang loud and clear in the small, crowded waiting room. In the car earlier, I had joined in with my mother's singing, but in this small room, one voice was more than enough. A couple of people stared at Mom, obviously not knowing what to think. Others peeked around or over the top of magazines wondering if this woman was sick or just plain silly. In the old days I would have been embarrassed by my mother's behavior, but after several years of dealing with Alzheimer's disease, I'd become much more resilient.

We were in the waiting room of the eye clinic, and it was a busy Wednesday. Mother had had cataract surgery a week earlier and it had not gone well. With the Alzheimer's it had been hard to explain to Mom how absolutely still she would have to be. She had become restless and they had not been able to complete the procedure. Parts of the cataract still needed to be removed and they had yet to replace the lens. The operating doctor thought we should see a specialist and try a different technique. So there we waited while she segued into "Amazing Grace."

I noticed a lady sitting beside Mom trying to fill out a long form. Mom's singing appeared to be affecting the woman's concentration. I told Mom to be quiet so the lady next to her could take care of her paperwork. Mom paused in her singing but then whispered in a voice loud enough for all in the office to hear, "How long do I have to be quiet?" Alzheimer's often returned Mom to her childhood, and I'd say right then she was eighty-five going on five years old. I saw some smiles on the faces of the folks sitting around us and was thankful for kind souls. About that time we were called into the treatment room. Mom sang her way down the hallway. "Just a Closer Walk With Thee."

I had been hopeful that the surgery would work, as Mom's eyesight had deteriorated with cataracts on both eyes. I was not sure if that was why she had quit reading or if she could no longer concentrate. I just wanted her to be able to see as clearly as possible even if her thinking had blurred.

What's surprising is that even in her confusion Mom could remember the words to so many songs. She loved music. I was grateful that part of her brain had been spared, at least for the time being.

She sang, "In the Garden" as we waited for the doctor to come in.

Mom's anxiety level was high. I felt terribly guilty though I knew it was unfounded. I had told her several times before the surgery that she would be able to see better after this procedure was done. I hadn't anticipated any problems. After the failed surgery, however, Mom could only see shadows. She was understandably paranoid. That day when I picked her up from the care facility, she had asked, "What are you going to do to me now?" I felt so bad. It was impossible to explain the procedure to her. There wasn't much I could say to comfort her after the fact. Instead, we sang along with *Elvis Sings Gospel* all the way into town. No other conversation was as comforting.

Through the progression of this disease, I was amazed by how Mom developed her own coping mechanisms—one of which was singing hymns. She sang constantly. On most occasions, I didn't try to stop or quiet her. God had left her that gift. Obviously, music soothed the Alzheimer's beast.

This whole cataract process took us about three weeks. During that time, Mom seemed to think of the hymns as prayers. Or maybe she just wanted to keep some noise going so she wouldn't think fearful thoughts. We will never know. What I do know is that we sang together often and in many different places for those three weeks. "Heavenly Sunshine," "How Great Thou Art," and "Just as I Am"—all had greater meaning to me by the time the ordeal was over.

The corrective surgery went well and Mom was able to see much better. At that point, doctors and family decided we would not try to correct the other eye. For once I was grateful for the forgetfulness caused by Alzheimer's. Mom wouldn't remember the fear and discomfort she had gone through. I was even more grateful to those great composers of the past whose hymns gave my mother a calming peace during this traumatic period.

44 The Doctor Visit

*W*ell *it feels like one of those days to mark on the calendar. It's not one you look forward to but one that shows a change in life.*

Mom had caught a case of the flu in early January. During the night, she had vomited on the floor and then tried to get up. In the process, she fell down. After observing her in the morning, the day caregiver made the decision to send her to the hospital for X-rays. We wanted no repeat of the broken hip a few years earlier, which had been a big part of her decline in health and mind. This time, thank goodness, nothing was broken. Even that same day when I visited Avamere she had already forgotten the hospital trip.

Three weeks later Mom wanted to depend *totally* on the use of the wheelchair. She was still complaining about a sore hip and leg—until she got to the doctor, that is. All of a sudden she was "fine." She couldn't understand why I'd taken her to the clinic. But that's typical Alzheimer's behavior.

The doctor asked Mom a few questions and then helped her stand and take a couple shaky steps. "Ruth is definitely favoring that leg," the doctor said. "I reviewed the X-rays again, and I see no break, but I see significant arthritis that might have been irritated." The doctor pressed in on both sides of Mom's hips trying to locate any tenderness. "Do you feel anything there?" the doctor asked. "Just fat," Mom responded matter-of-factly.

When I said I didn't want her to get used to using the wheelchair all the time, the doctor looked at me with understanding, asking, "And why is that, Bonnie? Is it for you or for her? You use the wheelchair for outings now, don't you? We should definitely encourage her to use the walker if she wants to, but she has the right to be fatigued, you know. If she is hurting, we shouldn't force her. It's not as if she's going to get better. I don't mean to sound cruel or uncaring; it is just the way this story goes."

I also expressed a concern that Mom was sleeping too much, not wanting to get out of bed in the morning. Patiently the doctor said, "She's getting tired. You have to accept that." I felt a little taken back. I didn't want to acknowledge what she was telling me.

She looked at Mom and said, "You have a wonderful quiet peacefulness about you today, Ruthie."

"I do?" Mom asked. "Well, I feel fine." They smiled at each other.

Inside I was having a little freak-out. It was great for them to have this little chat about Mom's "quiet peacefulness." What does that mean now? I thought. Quiet and peaceful were words I hadn't often heard used to describe my mother. Earlier in her life it was busy, restless, gypsy, vagabond; even later it was talkative, happy, smiling, open, and friendly. Never quiet. Never peaceful.

I guess it was *never say never* time.

Expectations had been lowered that day. Once again, I had to adjust my thinking and accept the process of Alzheimer's disease. Mom's health was calling the shots.

I didn't like it, but…oh well. It was time to get on the phone and let the family know what the doctor had had to say.

45 A Special Christmas Eve

O ur Christmas season had had its typical ups and downs. I was looking for another *up*. Though I knew the physical situation with Mom would be difficult, I was determined to take her to the Christmas Eve church service. I had been so pleased when I heard there was going to be an afternoon service. Taking her out at that time of day would be easier. The weather was terribly cold and windy. In retrospect, it almost made no sense to take Mom out, but I seemed driven to do so. I was grateful two of my sisters were there to help and to experience the effort it took to get Mom anywhere during those days.

As we arrived at the church, greeters helped Mom from the car to the wheelchair. It wasn't my habit to arrive at functions early, but on this day, we had given ourselves extra leeway. Once settled in the church, I was concerned that Mom would become restless or nervous about the strange surroundings and all the people moving about. In the past, no one was a stranger to her, and she had always loved people-watching. However, the word *always* had backfired on me more than once since Alzheimer's disease had taken over her life. This day she sat quietly in the wheelchair.

My sister Marge held Mom's hand and they exchanged quiet comments as we waited for the service to start. My sister Nancy and I made small talk until the lights went down and the now packed church quieted. I glanced at Mom to see that this was not going to cause uneasiness. She was fine. Carolers entered on each side of us. Soon Mom was singing along. I thought, *This is what I hoped for her.*

Though the congregation was asked to stand for prayer, Mom was not bothered. Quietly bowing her head in reverence, she seemed to feel at peace in knowing nothing was expected of her. We were in complete acceptance of our lives in that moment. We were there in celebration of the Christ child and felt the togetherness that family can bring.

The program continued with special musical productions. Mom particularly enjoyed the children, as we girls had expected. She listened contentedly through the pastor's message. As candles were lit, I wondered if she would be unsettled. Again she accepted what was going on around her with a contented expression.

At the end of the service, Mom was satisfied to let the crowd disperse before we guided her wheelchair toward the doors. I brought the car around and we were graciously helped with getting Mom into it. Her fear of falling had made the transition from wheelchair to car seat a difficult one. She had little sense of balance left. If she started to go down, I knew I could only cushion her fall, not stop it completely.

As much as we wanted Mom to have Christmas Eve dinner with us, we knew the outing to the church had been enough activity for one day. On the drive back to the care facility, Mom commented on the service. We had known she would enjoy the music and the children, but she appeared to be most impressed with the "preacher and his words."

"He's a very good talker," she repeated several times, "and he talked so sensible." I was pleased to know she felt blessed by the pastor's words. That was just an added bonus.

I chuckled to myself at the time, thinking *I'm sure Pastor Paul wouldn't let that compliment go to his head, considering ninety percent of her conversations are with her fellow Alzheimer's residents, many of whom are not one bit sensible.*

My sister Marge had come from Montana to spend the holidays at our home and to be able to have Christmas with Mom. She said her trip was worth it just to see the smile and the peacefulness on Mom's face during the service. It had been wonderful to share those moments with her. Nancy agreed; her trip in from Bend had been well worthwhile. Though our sister Shirley and our brother Russell could not be there, we felt blessed as a family. Holidays can be stressful for everyone, but blessings come from even the smallest shared family event.

46 More than Words Can Say

Eyes are the windows to the soul, I was thinking as I watched the two of them. *One set of eyes is disappointed and sad. The other set looks tired and empty.*

I've long been fascinated by people's eyes, but I'd rather not have seen what I saw that day. The beautiful blue eyes were those of my niece, Margie Ann. She was visiting from Montana, and this was the first time that her grandmother with Alzheimer's disease did not recognize her. It was a painful experience. She had known this day would come but had held on to the hope that it would not be this visit, not yet. Margie Ann was the first grandchild and one of her grandmother's favorites. She had held that identity while others had slipped away from her beloved Gramma Z. On that day, she did not see the love and pride that had been ever present there before. I could see the realization in her eyes: she could no longer share family news with her grandmother. Margie Ann would get no more words of encouragement or hope regarding the neuropathy affecting her feet more every day. She could not share the beautiful days she had just spent at the beach—nor any of the things she and her grandmother had loved to chat about in the past.

Her grandmother's hazel eyes looked at her with friendliness but not with recognition. They were almost blank, really, little expression at all. "Grandma, I'm Margie

Ann. I've come from Montana to visit you," she said in an almost desperate voice.

Grandma smiled. "That was nice of you," she answered politely. A year had passed since Margie Ann's last visit. It had been a long one for her grandmother; much more of her memory had evaporated.

A few minutes earlier my sister Marge had sat down beside Mom on the bench and said hello. Mom's face lit up a little then. "You look like someone who belongs to me," she had said. I'm sure she wouldn't have been able to come up with a name, but at least she knew that face. I saw relief in Marge's eyes and felt tears in my own.

"That's right, Mom, I belong to you. I'm Marge, your oldest daughter." It helped Mom recognize her but not enough to ask about Marge's husband or about their recent trip.

Conversation was difficult that day.

It was sad to watch as identity and connectivity were taken away from a woman who had held her family so dearly. Five children, fifteen grandchildren, twenty-five great-grandchildren, five great-great-grandchildren—all lost to her. I thought, *Now she sits alone on the bench in the Alzheimer's unit with no comprehension of how many people love her.* I wanted to shake her at times and try to wake her up. It was like she was in a vacuum. She felt only what was experienced in the moment, knew only what was real in the moment. How confusing and frustrating it must have been for her to look at a face and know she should have known who it was. It's hard to imagine the fear and loneliness she must have felt then.

Oh dear Heavenly Father, let me be faithful and know that you are watching over this precious woman. Let me be strong and know that someday I will have the eyes to see and understand your plan. Let me know that in your time you will take her in your loving arms away from this terrible disease. Let me know that her soul will be comforted and she will no longer be suspended in this cruel existence. Let her and me see the love in your eyes firsthand.

47 More than Words Part II

After I had written "More than Words Can Say," I sent it to my niece, Margie Ann. This, in part, was her reply:

Aunt Bonnie,

I sat down and cried at what you had written in your story about my last visit to Grandma Z. All I could think about was what my sister Trish had said to me before we left.

"Maybe you should put a little red in your hair before you go." At the time I thought, As if that's all Grandma Z could remember me by. *Well, now I think maybe that is true—since she didn't remember me. Here in Billings, my Grandma Heiser only knows or remembers me because of the candy I bring her. She remembers Dad because he wears his cowboy hat, and my mom because of her voice. There always seems to be something that triggers the memory.*

As I sit and watch my grandchildren at play, I pray I will always remember them. Memories are such a precious thing in life and we all take it for granted until we make one of those visits to grandparents in a nursing home.

How sad it is to live close to one hundred years and be unable to remember even one of them.

As you said when we were there, the Mom and Grandma we knew is gone. We are just waiting for this shell of a woman to go. I know I will never forget her eyes on that day; such dark, cold, empty eyes. Not at all like the eyes of the Grandma Z. we once knew and loved.

Give her a hug for me, even if she doesn't know who it's from.

With love, Margie Ann

Margie Ann had the misfortune of having both of her grandmothers in care facilities at the same time. Her grandmother here in Oregon suffered from Alzheimer's disease and her grandmother in Montana had dementia.

48 Aunt Gladys—Sister and Friend

My mother lost her best friend today and she doesn't even know it. I know how sad she would be, but I'll not tell her. My grief is doubled because it is hers and mine.

Mom's sister, my Aunt Gladys, died at age ninety. She was a wonderful woman, so happy and productive. As kids, we put our names on a list to get one of her monkey dolls made from men's socks. As we grew older, we stood in line for the crocheted doilies and colorful, cozy afghans. And she was a great cook. She made wonderful soups to warm cold winter days. People willingly drove across town to buy the raised donuts and twists served in the restaurant she and Uncle Rollie ran. Fragrant cinnamon rolls from her oven were a pure delight to friends and neighbors who stopped by for coffee.

Her heart was warm and loving, but she had a competitive spirit too. She could be downright wicked at dominoes, Aggravation, and card games. She is a treasured part of my childhood.

Aunt Glad's two sons were her pride and joy, but she had wanted daughters too, so she adopted my sisters and me as her own. Mom was more than happy to share her four girls, especially when Aunt Glad French-braided our hair and sewed dresses for us. My sister Nancy and I were tomboys and didn't entirely appreciate her dresses and sunsuits, but she insisted we needed them. Under direction from Mom, we wore them until she went home, then we were back in our T-shirts and jeans.

**Above, left to right:
Gladys age 17, Ruth
age 15.
Right, left to right:
Ruth age 19, Gladys
age 21.
Always best friends.**

Mom and Gladys both left formal schooling early to marry and raise families, so neither had high school diplomas. Aunt Gladys promised her sons that she would someday get her GED. At eighty-six years old, she decided she'd better get on with it. At eighty-seven she took part in a high school graduation in Superior, Wisconsin. Her sons walked proudly on each side of her wheelchair as she accepted her high school diploma to a standing ovation. She received a letter from Wisconsin's State Superintendent of Schools congratulating her on the accomplishment. Aunt Glad proudly sent me a copy to show to her favorite sister, Ruthie. Mom would have been so proud of her. I'm sure she would have attended the ceremony; unfortunately, Alzheimer's disease had progressed too far for Mom to understand what had happened or to experience the joy of that moment with her sister.

I remember a story Mom liked to tell about a nine-year-old boy who was her "school pal" in a program they had at the assisted living facility where Mom lived for several years before her Alzheimer's diagnosis. He had asked who Mom's best friend was, and her reply was, "It's always been my sister Gladys."

He was shocked. He said, "Are you sure? Sisters aren't usually best friends."

She told him, "Well, my sister is not the *usual* sister."

"Boy she must not be," he had replied shaking his head.

About a year earlier, Mom had become obsessed with the death of her mother, as if it just happened. She would cry inconsolably though my grandma died forty years earlier. She was upset that no one had told her that her mother was gone. She wondered if Grandma suffered. Was the funeral nice? Did anyone take pictures that she could see? It was a difficult time. Those who have experienced Alzheimer's disease could understand a call I got from a caregiver at Mom's facility. "Your Mom is upset tonight and having trouble getting to sleep. Could you talk to her and try to comfort her a bit?" she asked.

"Of course," I said. "What seems to be the problem?"

"Well, your grandmother died *again*." The caregiver said quietly. How cruel that Mom would have to live through that death anew over and over. All we could do was comfort her each time. Eventually my grandmother was put to rest even in my mother's mind.

My thoughts, like my mood, were heavy on that day. *I can't bring myself to tell Mom today that her sister is gone. I hope it's the right thing to do. I'm afraid she will be overcome with the loss and I can't put her through anything like that again.* Tears flooded my eyes as I hugged my mom, feeling the sadness and loss for both my aunt and my mother.

I know that Aunt Gladys had a strong Christian faith. There is no doubt she has gone to be with her Lord and Father. During her last days she asked for her "Little Margie," and Marge, my oldest sister, went to Wisconsin to be at her bedside. Their bond was that of mother and daughter. The doctors were giving Aunt Gladys morphine to ease her coughing attacks. As she awoke from one drug-induced nap, she looked at Marge and said, "Am I still here? I thought I'd be in heaven by now! You know your Uncle Rollie is waiting for me, and he's not a patient man!"

Marge answered, "I guess you'll have to stay with me a little longer. God must not be quite ready for you yet."

Several times during those last days Aunt Glad would ask her friend Kathy to read her favorite bible verse, Psalm 121:8. "The Lord shall preserve your going out and your coming in from this time forth and even forevermore." Aunt Gladys took such comfort in God's word. I wish Mom had been able to seek that comfort when Gladys died, but I doubt her clouded mind could take her to that place of peace by this time in her journey.

As I reflect on Mom's family, I can't help but wonder if Alzheimer's disease is genetic. Experts can only be sure about this in isolated cases. We have no history of it in our family before Mom. My aunt Gladys was bright and clearheaded to the end. Mom's other siblings were in their eighties and doing well mentally. My grandfather was singing Swedish hymns in his ninety-ninth year. On the other hand, Mom started showing signs of the disease at eighty years old. Just a twist of fate I guess; the luck of the draw. On the day of my aunt's death, my journal entry was brief.

In my prayers tonight I'll pray that God puts me on the same path as my Aunt Gladys and my Grampa Samuelson, not on the murky path of Alzheimer's that Mom has traveled. There will be a special prayer of thanks for the life of His faithful servant Gladys, and how much she meant to her younger sister and best friend Ruthie. My heart knows they will walk together again soon.

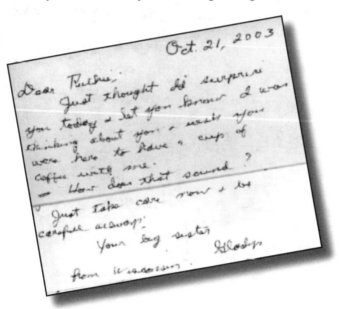

One of many notes from Ruth's big sister, Gladys. She tried to keep in contact with Ruth as they had always done, but unfortunately, Ruth was unable to respond.

Ruth and Duane on her visit to Augusta Georgia,
November 1982.

49 Duane Comes to Call

He was a man of strong stature. He carried his six-foot-two-inch frame like an ex-serviceman. Indeed, he had retired from the military and then gone into law enforcement. He had a stern manner about him, but his soft and caring eyes betrayed him. I had not seen my cousin Duane since I was five years old, nearly fifty-six years before.

He had come on a special visit. Duane hadn't seen his beloved Aunt Ruth for many years. The last six or seven years of suffering from Alzheimer's disease had not been kind to her. The once spirited, playful, loving woman sat in a wheelchair day after endless day, often lost in a world none of us could yet understand. Duane and his wife Marie had come from Augusta, Georgia, to see Ruth before the thick fog of Alzheimer's disease enveloped her completely.

There were seven of us visiting, too many to surround Mom at once, so only Duane and I walked up close to Mom's chair. The other five watched expectantly as he kneeled in front of her. I said, "Mom you have a visitor. It's Aunt Gladys's son, Duane. He has come a long way to see you."

She lifted her tired eyes to look at him and made her usual polite response. "Well that's nice." We were all quiet. Disappointment hung in the air. We had all hoped she would recognize him. As he knelt down in front of her, there was little change in the expression on her face. He told her again who he was and a bit about what he had been doing. It was hard to tell if she knew him or not. It looked as if he may have come too late.

"I'm sorry," I said to Duane as we left the facility.

He answered, "You have nothing to be sorry about."

"I know, but I had hoped she would remember. She cared so much for you."

"Oh, this was only the first visit," he said. "We planted the seed today. There is still time. I have more to talk to her about when there are not so many people to distract her." I loved his optimism.

The second visit did go better. Fewer people made it easier for Mom. I asked Duane if he knew any Swedish, Mom's native language. He said, "Boy, not much." So I suggested he sing something to her. He started with a few words from an old Swedish song, "Nikolina." With little change in her expression, Mom started mouthing the words along with him. There may have been little change in her face, but the rest of us were thrilled, especially Duane. He had opened a small door of remembrance. "She used to sing that song to me when I was a little boy," he said.

Duane's digital camera became quite the point of interest for Mom. He took a couple pictures of her then showed her the images. She watched his fingers pushing the buttons and soon her fingers were moving too, wanting to do it herself. He took another picture of her and me together. When she saw the shot of her alone, she asked, "Where's Bonnie?" She took the camera from his hands and starting pushing buttons until she saw the image she was looking for. She acted like a curious three-year-old with a new gadget. I immediately began thinking about which hand-held toy I could buy for her to "play" with—maybe one of those that my grandsons liked so well.

Years earlier Mom had visited Duane in Georgia when he was working as a special investigator. She had needed a change of scenery, so she hopped a Greyhound bus and rode the long miles from Superior, Wisconsin, to Augusta, Georgia. She had arrived late at night, and Duane picked her up at the bus station in his police car. He drove her around the city and told her about some of the nightlife. Even the seedier environments fascinated her. She loved the adventure while feeling safe and secure with her nephew, "the man in charge." It was a story she would tell many times over. As Duane reminded her of that visit, she smiled and made a remark about them "getting into mischief." It was clear she recalled something of the event. He had connected with her again.

On the third visit, Duane asked his wife if she would mind staying in the car while he visited with Ruth. Marie had a book in her bag and was content to sit in the warm sun and read. She would join us a little later. She knew what Duane was thinking. He wanted some one-on-one time with Ruth. Duane and I went into the facility. After we greeted Mom and took her out into the fresh air of the courtyard, Duane asked if I would mind leaving them alone. Of course it was fine with me. It felt good to have someone else take the role of encouraging conversation with Mom. I wandered off from the two of them, finding another bench to rest my weary bones and enjoy the sun. I looked on as they talked. It seemed that each time Duane visited Mom, she was more alert and able to communicate, even ask questions. Duane looked her directly in the eyes and spoke softly. I could see him prodding her to respond and she was doing well by the looks of it. He held her hand as he spoke to her. The gentleness of the moment was heartwarming. Such kindness and love is why God gave us families.

My brother Russell and his wife Helen went with Duane and Marie the following day on their last visit to Mom. In later conversation they said it had gone well. As they left the building, Duane had said, "I'm so glad I came here when I did. I dearly love that woman."

That was no surprise to hear after having watched him with her over the previous days. There is just not enough of that kind of love and respect in this world. Some folks at the facility with Mom never have a visitor. Many who do come are impatient, expecting too much. It is uncomfortable for others, not knowing what to say. It's not easy duty. But when a visitor comes in as Duane did, remembering their loved one as they once were, it is such a pleasure to see. Love and respect are the most wonderful gifts we can give to one another. Folks with Alzheimer's still want to be treasured.

I would guess Mom lost the memory of Duane's visit rather quickly, but I haven't.

Thanks, cousin.

From Mom's Journal:

> *We do not remember days, we remember moments.*
>
> —Cesare Pavese

50 Difficult Days

It became harder to visit. Mom rarely responded. She sat quietly and looked at me while I talked to her. I told her about family or what was going on, but her response was usually just a weak smile that was most likely an embedded polite reaction. I was grateful for even that, as many in the Alzheimer's unit were not so pleasant. As long as Mom could respond, she remembered to say thank you. Not a small thing.

I became seasoned to other happenings in the unit. I no longer gasped when I saw folks with nasty bruises. At the beginning of the journey, I wondered how the staff could "let" those things happen to the residents. I realized there was no way to watch each resident every minute, and the folks want to be active regardless of impaired balance. Barely a bump on a side table created a black and blue area. I remember an occasion when one of the other ladies looked like a raccoon. It seems she fell against her nightstand in the night, hitting right between the eyes, blackening both of them. These types of incidents are to be noted in the caregivers' desk logs. Families have access to these logs and should check out anything that looks suspicious. Though much bodily abuse is self-inflicted, I questioned the bumps and bruises, taking nothing for granted.

There is another side to that story too. Once when I came to visit, a male attendant showed me his red arms where Mom had continually slapped him while he tried to change her wet clothing. The female caregiver had gone home sick, and he was there alone for a couple hours. Mom had soiled her dress and he was trying to help her get into dry clothes. She wanted nothing to do with a male attendant helping her dress even though she knew him and liked him other than when it came to personal attention. He had been on staff for over a year and was wonderful with the residents. I apologized for her behavior but we both understood that she felt her space was being violated. I talked to the supervisor about calling in someone from the assisted living side to help when such things happened in the future. I felt they tried to accommodate the request.

One day I entered the facility to see an angry, nearly naked man having to be restrained by caregivers. He snarled liked a trapped animal and flailed his arms. I had never seen him that way in the months he had been at Avamere. No one was sure what had caused him to explode, but it was unsettling. The nurse had been called, and they were trying to calm him down and return him to his room. My sympathetic heart ached for his anger, confusion, and frustration. I said a desperate, silent prayer. *God please never let me have to see my mother like this.*

On the humorous side, one of the female residents was heard to say, "Just hit him over the head with a baseball bat. That will stop this!" She was not intimidated, but most of the others sat quietly, wide-eyed.

Many visits brought unexpected experiences. It's easy to become emotionally involved with the other residents and their trials as well as our own loved ones. It can often be overwhelming. In *Coping in New Territory: The Handbook for Children of Aging Parents,* author Suzanne Roberts gives another person's way of dealing with difficult visits. "I had a little mantra that I said each time I walked into the Alzheimer's unit: 'The light of God surrounds me, the love of God enfolds me, the power of God protects me, and the presence of God watches over me. Wherever I am, God is.' I wrapped myself in a white light, took a deep breath, and opened the front door with a greeting smile for the nursing staff."

Often we do not feel like visiting, but we must go. We cannot let it take us down. That's when grandchildren and happy recollections are such blessings to us who *can* remember. My husband frequently encouraged me, saying, "I know you don't feel like going today, but this might be one of Mom's good days and you'll miss it." He knew I couldn't pass up that opportunity.

51 A Special Donation

The thought kept nudging me as I read some material on Alzheimer's research. There were photos showing the brain in various stages of Alzheimer's disease. It had helped me to visualize the deterioration of the brain cells and connections. I could see that there were total dark spots in the brain, and what experts were referring to as "tangles."

This was great information. How did they get it all? Were these diagrams or were they actual pictures of brains? Did that mean with continuing research they would need more brain tissues donated? Uh-oh…something else to consider. My feelings were mixed, but nagging at me to dig deeper.

My mother was a curious woman, intrigued by research. She had participated in volunteer research studies on high blood pressure, and I believe another, years earlier at OHSU, was on lungs and breathing. I thought perhaps I should look into donating her brain, at the time of her death, to Alzheimer's research. I think she would have approved of that. She would have liked being part of another study conducted by the medical field she held in such high esteem.

Each of us has our own opinion and comfort level on these matters. Some people cannot imagine their loved one being "disassembled" for such a thing, seeing it as disrespectful. Others, like me, look at the body as a vessel to carry the spirit, which becomes nothing after the spirit has left it. Each view needs to be respected. I surely would not have moved forward with this precious donation if anyone in the family found it unacceptable, but I thought I should get the facts so I could pass on the correct information, if asked.

I was able to get a pamphlet from the Oregon Brain Bank at Oregon Health Sciences University (OHSU) called, *"How To Make Brain Tissue Donations For Research On Alzheimer's Disease And Other Dementing Illnesses."* It explained why and how donations are carried out. It talked about the costs and logistics of the procedure.

Another phone call gave me this emailed response from Senior Research Assistant Tracy Zitzelberger, of Oregon Health Sciences University:

"Thank you for your call about brain donation for your mother. I am sorry that we are not able to accept this tissue at this time, as we currently have ample tissue from patients with memory disorder. It sounds like your mother was an advocate for medical research and contributed to many kinds of research over the years. I greatly appreciate your interest in Aging and Alzheimer's research and would like to pass on some information about other groups that are involved in brain research."

With that she gave me information on Harvard Brain Tissue Resource Center (<www.brainbank.mclean.org> 1-800-Brain Bank [1-800-272-4622]) and Biogift Anatomical (<www. biogift.org> [503-670-1799]).

The logistics of donation got more complicated, and I chose not to go any further. I have no idea what is needed by the Oregon Brain Bank today, but I would assume such needs change often. It is an admirable and worthwhile undertaking for anyone who feels strongly about research. Current information can be requested from OHSU's Layton Aging and Alzheimer's Disease Center (<www.ohsu.edu/alzheimers/> [503-494-6976]).

I have to admit, I was relieved when our offer was not accepted. My head thought it was a good idea, but my heart couldn't follow through. I wasn't as strong as I thought I was.

52 Gift Wishes

It's interesting how our Christmas gift wishes change as the years go by. Little girls wish for dolls. Little boys ask for trucks or puppies. For teenagers it's new clothes or, these days, a whole array of electronic gifts to satisfy every desire. A couple of years later a car might top the wish list. Young marrieds set aside gift money for their new home.

As we get older, our gift wish often becomes less tangible. The gifts of time, peace, or family unity are likely to be more important.

This year as the holidays approached I could not put together a Christmas gift wish. I knew it would be an emotional year because Mom had faded even further into the clouds of Alzheimer's. It would be the first Christmas that she would not be able to give me a holiday greeting or sing the age-old Christmas carols she loved. I truly thought she would not make it to this holiday season. She was still with us. What other gift could I wish for?

As it turned out, an afternoon social event gave me the answer to the question and the gift itself.

Susan and Terry, two of the caregivers at Avamere, wanted to do something special for the residents during the holiday season. It is often difficult to get family members to participate in social functions, but they felt it was worth the effort. Invitations were sent out.

Terry was from the Philippines. She was working here in the United States to make enough money to build a church in her home country. She loved holiday music and wanted to have a small Christmas program given by the residents. She often led the Sunday sermons so she was aware the folks liked to sing hymns. She had thought, why not have a Christmas choir? They began practicing weeks before the party.

When the day arrived, my niece, Lori, and nephew, Wes, joined me at their grandmother's celebration. I appreciated their company, as Mom didn't have much to say these days. This time the party was well attended. The caregivers had done a great job. There were festive decorations and many wonderfully tempting snacks lined up on the counter. Terry led her choir through several familiar carols and those able joined in the singing. It was a special time. For a few minutes we were just families enjoying the season together. I suspect that no one was thinking of the debilitating disease that is Alzheimer's.

After the singing, to my great surprise, Terry asked a resident if he would lead us in prayer for the food we were about to eat. Mr. McGrew had been a teacher and missionary in his earlier years, a true man of God. He had been at Avamere for several months and was steadily losing conversational skills. I wondered why she would put him on the spot like that. Obviously she knew him better than I. He asked if he was supposed to pray for his wife. She reminded him he was to say grace over the food. I so wished I had a recording of his beautiful, thoughtful prayer. Only once did he get off track and say something about "getting into a car." His heartfelt honest blessing was an amazing tribute to God's goodness. I can't begin to write it in the loving, adoring way he said it. As we all joined the "Amen," I don't think there were many dry eyes in the place. My niece and I looked at each other's tear-filled eyes and laughed a bit, overwhelmed with emotion. Mr. McGrew may have been confused by most of his life that day, but he knew how to pray to his Father in heaven.

After eating, we were entertained by an accordion player. The musician was a pleasant woman who often performed at the facility. Her familiarity put the residents at ease. She asked if anyone wanted to dance. Several of the residents danced uninhibited. It was fun to see. When a waltz was played, a gentleman asked his wife, one of the residents, to dance. Often a troubled, crying woman, she was transformed to a smiling young lady dancing with the love of her life. There was no question these two had danced together for many years. We all watched, totally caught up in the graceful movement.

Again sentimental tears welled. How wonderful that these two could enjoy a few minutes of happiness: a Christmas gift-wrapped in memories.

Mom didn't seem to see them dancing. Maybe it was too painful to acknowledge her inability. How she had loved to dance and now was no longer able to stand without assistance. From her wheelchair, I hope she felt some warmth of the moment.

Lori and Wes were both impressed with the sincere enjoyment displayed that afternoon. My nephew said, "Now I see why you spend time here. I see where your blessings come from." He was right.

As the party wound down, they left to attend a birthday party for a sweet little boy celebrating his first birthday. What a contrast that would be to those at Avamere, closer to the end of life and hanging tight to each pleasant moment.

In the end I guess my Christmas wish was that Mom would recognize and enjoy the day. I'm not sure she did. I know she was at the party and there was much love in that room. I longed for "Merry Christmas" from her one more time but I had to be satisfied with a faint smile as I kissed her forehead and told her I loved her.

My gift was for us to be together and to share her last Christmas.

53 *Goodbye*

I was going to end my book about Mom with her passing on January 19, 2005. Then the more I thought about it, the more I knew I couldn't do it. In all that I have written, I wanted to pass on precious moments to be cherished. In remembering my mother there should be no sorrow and sadness. That is not what her life was all about. So I feel I should relate how it really ended—in a spirit of celebration.

First of all, let me tell you that I was scared of her dying. I had never seen a person die before, and this was my precious mother. When Avamere called my home at 2:30 in the morning, I knew this was going to be it. Nancy, her husband, and her son had been to see Mom the day before, but they were long gone back to Bend. The caring hospice people had told us then that Mom probably had three or four more days at the most. There would be no more food and no more medications given. Mom looked peaceful and quiet, and I was counting on those three or four days. My other sisters were coming in from Billings, Montana, and from Baker City, Oregon, and my brother from Yuma, Arizona, but none were going to be able to get here for a day or so. The ringing phone told me we were out of time. It was going to be Jim and me.

Even though Mom had been in a sleep mode most of the last few days, I had been told to continue to talk to her. Hearing is the last sense to go, they say. Hospice staff encouraged us to tell her how much we loved her and anything else we wanted her to know before she left this earth. Once I got comfortable with that, I was able to tell her what a wonderful person she had been, that she had taught us all well, and that her family was doing fine. I told her not to be afraid, that Jesus was going to be there with his hand reaching for hers, that she would not be alone. I whispered Psalm 23 to her. Only once that last day was I able to get her to open her eyes. I told her, "It's Bonnie, Mom; I'm here to see you." No response. "Open your eyes, Mom." Still, no response. In a louder, more authoritative voice—the one she called my "mean voice"—I said, "Ruthie, your baby girl is here to see you." Her eyes opened and she gave me a faint smile. "Oh yes," is all she said, and closed her eyes again. That is the last look I got from her with any recognition. I was glad, too, that Nancy, Vic, and Otto had been able to talk to her. Nancy said that Mom's eyes focused on her once, but then she seemed to be looking past her. The hospice lady commented, "She's looking past this world now and on to the next." That was comforting to hear.

I wondered, then, as we drove to Avamere in the darkness, "Would she have a few moments of being awake before she passed? Would there be any last words? How will this be? Will I be able to handle it? I was ever so thankful for my husband at that moment. He had been so supportive these last five years of being responsible for Mom's care. He had stood beside Mom with love and respect. *Thank God he is here again helping me through this difficult process of letting go.*

When we reached the facility, it was dreadfully quiet. Mom's roommate was curled up sleeping on the couch in the living room. It was not an unusual sight but somehow foreboding that night. As we walked to Mom's room, caregivers repeated the phone message. "She is not responding at all, her breathing has become heavy, and we believe she is in her last stage." Thoughts *circled in my head and heart. What happened to my three or four days? I wish my siblings were here. How are they going to feel about not being able to get here in time? I can't worry about that. I'm here to be with my mother to say once again all the things I told her the days before and this time to say good-bye.*

Though Jim and I are not Catholics, we honored the requests of family members who are by summoning a priest to administer her last rites. At 4:30 AM Mom stopped breathing. No fuss, no discomfort, no moments of last awakening. She simply stopped breathing. Strange how the sound of breathing is barely noticeable in life, but at the time of death the lack of it creates a screaming silence. It was not horrible or scary. It was simply a passing from one life to another, quiet and peaceful. Jim held me close. I was okay.

Mom was gone.

Jim went home to call the family. I called my nephew Evan and asked him to come and pray with me. He said his mother was to arrive in Portland at 6 AM and that his sister was picking her up and coming straight to Avamere. He would be there as soon as he could. I stayed beside Mom.

The caregivers came in one by one to say good-bye to Mom and to give me hugs. As I waited for someone from the funeral home to come for Mom, the shift changed. The next crew of caregivers came in to cry with me. Most truly care for the folks they work with. I don't know how they do it. I am forever grateful to those who cared for Mom. They took time to figure out her personality and work with her—incredible people.

As some residents started to stir in the hallway, I heard Mom's friend Sam say, "Are you okay, Ruthie? Is everything okay in there? Are you coming out soon?" I couldn't bring myself to face him just then. One of the caregivers guided him into the dining room.

An hour and a half passed before the fellow from the funeral home came. He had formalities to take care of which took a few minutes. I told him my sister was on her way and asked if he could possibly delay taking Mom for a few minutes longer. He was so kind saying, "There is no reason to rush." Soon after, my sister, niece, and nephew all arrived at once. They were glad to be able to say good-bye and pray together for Mom.

Mom had saved us much of the grief of planning a funeral for her. Paperwork was in place. The prepaid plan answered most of the questions, so when my sisters arrived, we were able to finish the necessary arrangements easily. What was most important was that this should be a time of remembering who Mom was and what a full life she had lived.

The bottom line was this: we would dress Mom in her best red suit, she would wear matching *very* red lipstick, and that tube of lipstick would be in her hand as she was sent away. This was a good thing as it turned out, because later a great-granddaughter was heard to say, "I'm so glad they put that red lipstick on Gramma. If they hadn't, I would have!" We would play hymns like "The Old Rugged Cross" and "How Great Thou Art" as people were seated. There would be an afghan made by Mom's beloved sister, Gladys, placed on the casket. We would do the flowers ourselves using colors and flowers we knew she loved. We would not wear dark colors and be mournful. After the funeral there would be lots of good food. Mom's grandson, Wes, would barbecue ribs just the way his grandmother had liked them. There would be lots of beans, salads, pickles, and desserts. All the things Mom had so enjoyed would be served. The theme was: wear red, listen to country music, and eat good food.

People are so kind and generous. Food, flowers, and offers of help started coming to our house. The phone took only short breaks from ringing. Our house is usually quiet, so with the company arriving one, two, or four at a time, it felt a bit overwhelming.

Emotions ran high. Each person had his or her expectations. Sadly, we were not able to get through it all without some conflict, but that's the nature of families, I guess.

The funeral went as well as funerals can go. Mom's grandson Evan led the service and handled the music. He had agreed months earlier to take care of all that, and I so appreciated his help. We sent her off with "Will the Circle be Unbroken" and then "Wings of a Dove." You have to know old country music to know those songs, but many of us could easily visualize Mom dancing around the kitchen singing them with a grandchild or two in her arms.

The oldest daughter, Marge, thanked all who had come and all who had cared for Mom in any way over the years. Shirley spoke of the good times she and Mom had shared in days gone by. Nancy had written a wonderful poem on her way back to Bend after seeing Mom for what she knew would be her last visit. Her words lovingly expressed what many of us had often thought through the years as Mom suffered with Alzheimer's disease.

Where Has My Mother Gone?

I sit in front of Mom and search her face
But she is gone to another place
The face I see I know so well
Looks back at me in the mirror and on the
faces of my brother and sisters
My mother the gypsy is off wandering
I hold her hand, still so fine. The skin so
delicate—tissue thin

Where are you, Mother?
Ever ready to go at the drop of a hat
I know when the Alzheimer's started, you
fought to stay this time
We could feel the fear and anger and clung
to each brief clear spell
We can't talk about the memories, but my
mind carries me there
My face is lined now, too, but when I don't
feel well I think of Mom
and of comfort food—mine was crackers
and milk
Of Mom's hand on my forehead, of her
sacrifices and hard work
I often think of Mom as a bird with a
broken wing
Wanting to fly but held back by a fear of
not being good enough
Of being born before her time
I know she loved us all. She wanted us to
fly like she couldn't
Kids, grandkids, great- and great-great-
grandkids: Show what you can do
Where are you Mom?
Can I hope God has let your mind free?
Can I hope you are off flying at last?
The body we hover around no longer holds
that spirit we all know you have
I hope it is flying around the country
dancing in the clouds and looking over us
all

Where have you gone Mom?
I hope you are out dancing
I love you Mom
—Your daughter Nancy
January 18, 2005

Wow. Amazing words.

It was my turn to speak, and I found myself hard-pressed to stay composed after that beautiful piece. I looked around and could see her still among us, her characteristics showing up in us, her children, grandchildren, and great-grandchildren. My heart spoke of the legacy left by our mother. *I see those with Mom's wonderful sense of adventure and love of travel. I see people who love other people, airports, shoes, reading, and dancing. I see people who work hard and take pride in a job well done. I see others eager to learn, who gather books around themselves, ready to take part in the great adventure of life. I see spirit and strength and simple joy. I see a blonde-haired boy who reminds of us our Swedish heritage. She has not gone from us. She has left a lot to live up to. Her life should be a challenge to the rest of us. Wear red! Sing out loud! Eat good food! Dance! Love your family! Work hard! Find joy! Be happy!*

Hers was a life to celebrate.

The gathering was over. There was too much food, as usual. So much kindness, so much love had been shown but now folks needed to go home. Our house grew quiet again. Marge stayed an extra few days to help me adjust and to finish any business.

At her request, Mom was cremated. When they called to say her ashes were ready to be moved to Willamette Cemetery, we were prepared. It was a beautiful day, just as we had hoped. At the funeral parlor, we picked up the metal container and put it in the box Jim had built for Mom with love and care. The red cedar was polished satin smooth; the hand carved hearts carefully placed. The funeral director asked if we wanted him to carry the ashes. Marge said in a firm tone, "No, I'll carry my mother." We got in the car, loaded the CD of Hank Williams, and headed to the cemetery. Down the freeway we went singing "Hey, Good Lookin'" at the top of our voices. No funeral procession here. Not for our mother!

Mother's ashes were buried at Willamette Cemetery in the same site as her late husband Joe. She had often said, "Put me there with Joe. I have unfinished business with that man!"

Look out Joe! Here comes Ruthie, and she's going to be ready to dance.

Closing note: Alzheimer's disease takes away so much from a person's last years, but we must not give up on that person too soon. Long after the diagnosis is given, there are still so many *moments this good* to cherish.

54 *What We Learned*

This journey is not an easy one. It only has one ending. Every person afflicted with Alzheimer's disease will take the journey in his or her own way. The problem is that even as we learn how to handle one issue, a new one arises. What I've done here is simply share some of the things our family learned as we went through the eight years in which we watched our happy-go-lucky, friendly mother fade into Alzheimer's disease. It was heartwarming and heartbreaking. There's nothing to do but get through it, gently and intact. Allow me to share a few things that might help anyone beginning this journey.

Recognizing the onset

Forgetfulness ... disorientation ... inability to do simple daily tasks ... not eating even when there is food in the refrigerator ... not answering phone calls, or making phone calls one after another ... mail unattended, bills unpaid ... paranoia ... repetitive conversation ... medications over- or underused ... unsociability ... sleeping too much ... losing things ...seclusion ... hoarding ...

Getting a diagnosis

Find a doctor who works with the older population if possible ... stay positive ... be realistic ... involve all family members ...

accept what you are told about Alzheimer's disease, but do not accept hopelessness ... consider all options ... don't feel guilty ... start gathering and reading all information available ... call the Alzheimer's Association for resources ...

Home care

Call the Alzheimer's Association to find a support group ... read *The 36-Hour Day: A Family Guide to Caring for Persons With Alzheimer's Disease, Related Dementing Illnesses, and Memory Loss in Later Life*, by Nancy L. Mace ... know your limitations ... have a backup "sitter" ... remove unsafe items from your home, much as you would for a small child ... be aware of when to lock doors ... do not leave your loved one alone ... avoid loud noise, commotion, and confusion ... never argue with someone suffering from Alzheimer's disease ... get as much rest as possible ... serve well-balanced, simple meals ... watch what your loved one helps himself or herself to on the table ... know you can't be perfect ... spend quality time even if it's coloring ... reminisce about family, friends, and places—it's the short-term memory that's gone ... music works wonders with many ... have a little girl polish fingernails ... slather hands and arms with a fragrant lotion ... keep a cozy afghan close by ... have someone come in to give you a break for a few hours a week ... do easy puzzles ... cutting out coupons from the Sunday paper can be an activity ... some folks like folding simple laundry items ... some like helping with cooking projects—Mom loved picking grapes off the vine when I was making grape juice ... find a daycare facility for a couple afternoons a week ... recognize when it's time for twenty-four-hour facility care ... again, don't feel guilty ... your loved one will only be well and safe if *you* are well and safe ... read *The Best Friends Approach to Alzheimer's Care*, by Virginia Bell and David Troxel ...

Looking for a facility

Again, Alzheimer's Association can help ... find a facility nearby for convenience—there will still be plenty for you to do ... short hallways are easier ... soft colors on the walls ... pictures at eye level ... check out the activities calendar ... glance over the menu ... stay for a meal ... check resident-to-caregiver ratio ... look at the rooms—simple is better ... how many per room ... is there a nurse on staff? ... cleanliness of facility and residents ... consider what you can afford knowing high dollars are no guarantee of the best care ... consider foster care with fewer residents ... a fenced yard or courtyard is great for exercise on warm spring days ...

Moving in to stay

Take something familiar like a lamp or bedspread ... pictures of family are nice—but not your only copy ... identify eyeglasses and even dentures ... take washable, comfortable clothes—you can bring in special clothes for special occasions ... use permanent markers to label clothing ... go through the closet occasionally to replace worn-out items or perhaps return items to the correct owner ... cardigan sweaters are nice for the chilly days ... sweaters with pockets work well for hankies, but don't be surprised what else might show up—like puzzle pieces or bingo squares ... speaking of puzzles, never bring one to the Alzheimer's unit with more than twenty pieces ... in an Alzheimer's facility room doors are seldom locked, so don't bring in anything precious or expensive for your loved one's room; it may disappear ... find a way to identify your person's walker—they all look alike. Permanent marker or stick-on nametags work well. We bought our mother a red one ... be kind and respectful to everyone: doctors, lawyers, housewives, and missionaries are all living here. Don't be condescending ...

bring in a treat once in a while—a favorite cookie or candy or even pickles if it's okay with staff. I took in slices of apples and pears when they were ripe. It's surprising what conversation it might encourage ... stay for supper once in a while ... go in for the singing programs and encourage everyone to sing along. I learned it didn't matter that my voice is not the greatest—the residents loved it when I joined in ... go to where your loved one's mind is on any particular day: young girl, new mother, sister, or friend. Just jump in and enjoy the fun ... don't consider any resident a mental case—all levels of education, vocations, and lifestyles are represented in an Alzheimer's wing. I have heard it said that "age and illness are the great levelers in society" ... talk to all the residents. There are some great stories to be heard ... keep your visit pleasant ... did I mention *never argue with a person who has Alzheimer's?* ... it's better to visit often than to stay too long ... be conversational; don't just ask questions: they can be confusing and intimidating ... say who you are just in case they cannot remember on any particular day ... monitor medications ... be the advocate ... get to know the staff and ask questions of them ... see if anyone comes in to clip and clean toenails—it makes for healthier feet and it's a treat for your loved one ... bring flowers from your garden ... join the facility support group ...

Outings

Some folks like outings, some don't: remember the personality of the person *before* Alzheimer's disease ... Mom loved to come to my house for lunch ... a drive in the country is often enjoyable ... keep the length of the outing appropriate for the resident ... church services are enjoyable for some, especially if they've been a long-term attendee ... outings can be a good stimulant. Mom often thought clearer while out among the family, but too many people around may prove overwhelming

... seeing animals might be a popular outing: find someone who has horses or puppies or a llama farm ... McDonald's can be fun for kid-watching ... keep outings simple ... keep a piece of candy in the glovebox ... keep a rag doll in the car for company ...

Other thoughts

A person's depth perception could be impaired, making stairs frightening ... dark-colored rugs might look like deep holes ... a person may not know when to stop eating or may eat too much of one thing (like the condiments!) ... use common sense ... be polite and respectful ... give much love love love, no matter what ...

"Thief"
From *Mosaic Moon,* by Frances H. Kakugawa

Before the thief came
I saw her with all the flaws of an imperfect mother.
I became righteous and judgmental
In my quiet unspoken perception of her.

Then the thief came quietly into the night
Like that fog on little cat feet
And slowly began to rob her
Of what was rightfully hers since her birth.
> Childhood memories
> Dates and places.
> Yesterdays and todays
> Even family faces.
Oh so quietly so silently
Stolen without a sound.

A woman struggling each day to retain
What little dignity the thief had not found
In the tiny remaining crevices of her mind.

My heart aches with love
For the woman she has become.

Perhaps there is a reason for the thief.

The mother is no longer here
But a shell of a woman
Leaving me nothing to judge nothing at all.
She sits for hours without a past without a present

A final transformation of a mother
Into her purest form
A newborn babe once again
Before her final journey

Permission to print from "Mosaic Moon: Caregiving Through Poetry"
©Frances H. Kakugawa.
Watermark Publishing, Honolulu, Hawaii
(www.bookshawaii.net)

This poem articulates my story well. By the end of this journey into Alzheimer's disease, my faith in God had increased tenfold and my mother had become my hero.

Appendix 1
The Brain

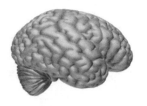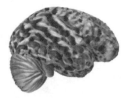

Shown above is a very graphic example of how Alzheimer's disease attacks the brain. One image is of a healthy brain. The other shows the brain with advanced Alzheimer's. Note how dramatically the brain has shrunk in total size, affecting nearly all its functions. The shadowed areas are a result of cell death and tissue loss. *Photos courtesy the Alzheimer's Association.*

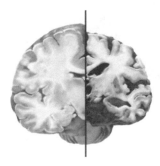

This picture is a "slice" of the healthy brain and the brain affected by Alzheimer's disease. Seeing this example shows us how much of the healthy brain is lost. It becomes very clear why thinking, planning, remembering old information and forming new memories are beyond the scope of those suffering from this disease. *Photo courtesy the Alzheimer's Association.*

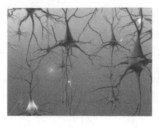

The photo on the left shows healthy nerve cells in the brain tissue. The other shows how abnormal clusters of protein, called plaque, build up between nerve cells. Another protein makes up twisted strands of dead and dying nerve cells called tangles. Both affect the functionality of the brain. *Photos courtesy the Alzheimer's Association.*

This information and more is shown on the website www. alz.org/brain (See "Inside the Brain:An Interactive Tour"). Another great source for understanding how the brain is affected by Alzheimer's is *Understanding Alzheimer's Disease,* by Neal R. Cutler, M.D. and John J. Sramek, Pharm D.

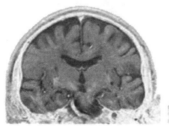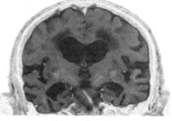

Left side brain: 92 year old male—cognitively healthy. Right side brain: 92 year old male—severe Alzheimer's disease. *From the Oregon Brain Aging Study, Oregon Health Sciences University, Portland, Oregon. Used by permission.*

Appendix 2

A Few Words about the Alzheimer's Association

Today five million people in America suffer from Alzheimer's disease. With age being the primary cause of Alzheimer's, and each generation living longer, that number will climb. Alzheimer's has no respect for nationality, gender, education, or financial stability.

Those facing Alzheimer's, daily find a difficult world. Some people are fortunate enough to be able to stay in their homes. Others are moved to Alzheimer's care facilities as the disease progresses. Whatever the situation, the Alzheimer's Association can offer help to those seeking to understand and cope with the disease.

ॐ **Helpline:** Care consultation, information, and referral are available. The helpline is open 24 hours a day toll free (800.272.3900 or TDD: 866.403.3073), or feel free to email at info@alz.org.

ॐ **Support groups:** Be referred to a support group in your area providing emotional support and education.

ॐ **Education:** Education and training programs are offered for family and professional caregivers.

ॐ **Safe Return Program:** An enrollment program, available 24 hours a day, that helps locate and return individuals who have wandered and become lost.

ชื Books, videos, and pamphlets: The Association has books, videos, and pamphlets with information on Alzheimer's disease, caregiving, and family issues, available for check out.

ชื Online:

www.alz.org/oregon
Look for "Inside the Brain: An Interactive Tour" online.
Alzheimer's Association
Oregon Chapter
1311 NW 21st Avenue
Portland, OR 97209

> *We will miss you Gramma Z, but now Grampa Joe has you to dance with again and that makes all of us happy.*
> *Love Tamara, Neil, Sevien and Ari*

This personal message, sent with flowers from Ruth's granddaughter and family, seemed to sum up how many of us were feeling when Ruth's journey here on earth came to an end.

More Praise for *Moments This Good:*

In *Moments This Good*, Nester tenderly chronicles her mother's Alzheimer's, bravely sharing with the reader the ways she and her family managed to transform the suffering and grief the disease causes—as loved ones recede from view in the memory of the Alzheimer patient. Nester offers the reader a path to gentle acceptance, and even moments of playfulness and joy—and always, always models profound love and respect for her mother. This fine little book lightens the load Alzheimer's can put on any family and makes an important contribution to a deeper understanding of the disease.

—Ellen Waterston
Author of the award-winning memoir *Then There Was No Mountain* and *I Am Madagascar*, winner of the 2005 WILLA Poetry Award. Waterston is the founder and director of the Writing Ranch and The Nature of Words.

There is a loss and grief that comes years before a funeral when a loved one suffers from dementia. Bonnie opens her experience to all of us as we share her pain, delight in her humor and gain strength when she offers solutions to problems we could barely define. Bonnie sees the "glass as half full" which reminds each of us that each moment can hold a gift for us in its hand.

—Suzanne Roberts
Author of *Coping In New Territory, The Handbook for Children of Aging Parents*